Machine Learning Unraveled

Exploring the World of Data Science and AI

Alex Murphy

Table of Contents

INTRODUCTION

The fields of AI and algorithms for learning have been developing at an exponential rate in recent years, changing several businesses as well as the way we live. Artificial Intelligence has had a significant and wide-ranging impact on a variety of fields, including marketing, finance, healthcare, and autonomous systems. Providing insights for both novices and seasoned professionals, "Machine Learning Unraveled: Exploring the World of Data Science and AI" is intended to be your entire guide to these revolutionary technologies.

The development of AI and machine learning dates back to the middle of the 20th century when pioneers like Alan Turing created the framework for contemporary computing. Since then, substantial advancements in computer science, statistics, and data accessibility have come together to produce complex algorithms that can learn from data and make well-informed predictions. It must be understood to fully understand this historical context in order to appreciate the current situation and foresee future developments.

Fundamentally, data science is an interdisciplinary area that extracts knowledge from both structured and unstructured data using scientific systems, algorithms, and procedures. Forming the core of machine learning, this field combines domain-specific knowledge, computer science competence, and statistics skills to manage and analyze large datasets. Creating efficient machine learning models requires having a solid understanding of data preprocessing, cleaning, and analysis.

Algorithms that can learn from data and get better over time are created through machine learning, a branch of artificial intelligence. Generally speaking, these algorithms fall into three categories: reinforcement learning, unsupervised learning, and supervised learning. Labeled data is used in supervised learning to train models for categorization or prediction. On the other hand, unsupervised learning finds inherent structures or hidden patterns in unlabeled data. Reinforcement learning, which is frequently applied in robotics and gaming, focuses on teaching agents to make a sequence of decisions by rewarding desired actions.

A strong ecosystem of tools and technologies supports the field. Python and R are popular languages because of their ease of use and robust library systems. Platforms like Jupyter Notebook and Google Colab offer interactive interfaces for data exploration and model construction, while frameworks like TensorFlow, Scikit-learn, and PyTorch provide the infrastructure needed to build and distribute models.

A range of techniques for regression and classification tasks are part of supervised learning. Building predictive models requires the use of logistic regression, decision trees, k-nearest neighbors (k-NN), support vector machines (SVM), and linear regression. By merging several models, ensemble techniques like bagging and boosting increase model accuracy. Innovative methods like neural systems and deep understanding (DL) have revolutionized machine vision and the processing of natural languages (NLP).

Unsupervised learning methods like dimensionality reduction and grouping are handy for finding hidden patterns in data. Similar data points are grouped together using clustering algorithms like k-means and hierarchical clustering, while high-dimensional data is simplified by dimensionality reduction methods like principal component analysis (PCA).

This book explores advanced subjects like computer vision, reinforcement learning, natural language processing, time series analysis, and recommender systems, which go beyond these fundamental ideas. These fields offer a wealth of opportunities, ranging from the development of intelligent agents to the comprehension of human language and the analysis of temporal data.

There are many real-world uses for machine learning. It helps with drug development, personalized medicine, and predictive analytics in the healthcare industry. It improves fraud detection, credit scoring, and algorithmic trading in the financial sector. While autonomous systems like self-driving cars and drones rely on machine learning for real-time decision-making, marketing uses it for client segmentation, churn prediction, and personalized suggestions.

As we use machine learning, it is crucial that we address ethical issues like prejudice, fairness, and privacy concerns. It is crucial for the future to create AI systems that are not just strong but also morally and fairly distributed.

"Machine Learning Unraveled: Exploring the World of Data Science and AI" will lead you through basic ideas, cutting-edge methods, and valuable applications to give you a thorough grasp of this ever-evolving topic. This book will provide you with the information and abilities to successfully traverse the always-changing field of machine learning and artificial intelligence, regardless of where you are in your path or how advanced you want to get.

CHAPTER I

The Evolution of Machine Learning and Data Science

The origins and early history of machine learning
The genesis and preliminary chronicles of machine learning are intricately linked to the wider advancement of computer science and artificial intelligence (AI). The field of machine learning is a topic of computer science that focuses on developing statistical models and algorithms that use inference and patterns to allow computers carry out certain jobs without explicit guidance. The development of machine learning into what it is today is the result of a complex interweaving of theoretical advancements, real-world uses, and visionary scientists.

Early in the 20th century, machine learning first emerged conceptually. Mathematicians and logicians like Alan Turing were fascinated by the idea of a machine that might replicate human intelligence. The "Turing Test," which is a standard for judging whether a computer is capable of intelligent behavior that is comparable to or indistinguishable from human behavior, was first proposed by Alan Turing in 1950. The notion that robots would be able to learn and adapt was a significant intellectual advance that laid the foundation for later advancements in artificial intelligence and machine learning.

In the 1940s and 1950s, several notable people made significant contributions to the development of the machine learning foundations. Warren McCulloch and Walter Pitts initially presented artificial neural networks in their 1943 paper "A Basic Theory of Ideas Present in Neurological Activity." Their model was made up of essential neurons that could be connected to construct networks and carry out intricate calculations. This was a forerunner of the neural networks that are currently utilized in machine learning.

The theoretical foundations of machine learning were greatly aided by another influential person, Claude Shannon, who is frequently referred to as the father of information theory. The foundation for comprehending and processing information was established by Shannon's work in the late 1940s, and this is essential for creating algorithms that can learn from data. His 1950 study, "Programming a Computer for Playing Chess," foreshadowed the use of algorithms in machine learning by examining the possibility of robots to carry out activities usually associated with human intelligence.

Several vital ideas in machine learning were formalized in the 1950s and 1960s. In 1959, industry pioneer Arthur Samuel came up with the term "machine learning". A fundamental tenet of machine learning was proven by Samuel's work on creating a checkers-playing program, which showed that computers might get better over time without human assistance. His definition of machine learning is still widely understood to mean "the discipline of research that provides machines the capacity to acquire knowledge without being explicitly programmed."

During this time, significant advancements were made in the development of models and algorithms that could interpret data and draw conclusions from it. The 1958 discovery of the perceptron by Frank Rosenblatt was revolutionary. An artificial neural network called a perceptron was created to categorize inputs into distinct groups, mimicking the essential functions of organic neurons. Even with its drawbacks, the perceptron paved the way for more advanced neural network models to appear in the decades that followed.

The discipline of machine learning kept developing in the 1960s and 1970s thanks to developments in theory and application. Thomas Cover and Peter Hart's 1967 invention of the nearest neighbor algorithm was one crucial advancement. Pattern recognition and classification jobs have come to rely heavily on this technique, which groups data points according to the classes of their closest neighbors.

Larger datasets and more complicated models could be tested by academics thanks to the 1970s' introduction of more potent computers. Around this time, Ryszard Michalski proposed the idea of inductive inference, which substantially broadened the theoretical underpinnings of machine learning. A key component of learning from data is creating algorithms that can generalize from particular instances to more general norms, which is the emphasis of Michalski's work.

The field of machine learning research saw substantial expansion and diversification in the 1980s. Artificial neural network training was completely transformed in 1986 when David Rumelhart, Geoffrey Hinton, and Ronald Williams popularized the backpropagation technique. Backpropagation solved many of the drawbacks of previous models, such as the perceptron, by enabling the effective modification of weights in multi-layer networks. Future developments in deep learning will be made possible by this innovation, which will make it possible to create neural networks that are more sophisticated and powerful.

In that same decade, decision tree learning emerged in the discipline; one prominent example is Ross Quinlan's ID3 method. Decision trees added a simple and understandable technique to the machine learning practitioner's practical toolkit for tasks involving regression and classification.

Machine learning as a discipline matured and became more and more applied to real-world situations in the 1990s and early 2000s. Vladimir Vapnik and his associates developed support vector machines (SVMs), which have now grown to be an effective tool for regression and classification. SVMs were a popular option for many applications because of their strong performance and theoretical guarantees.

Machine learning models' capabilities were significantly strengthened by the emergence of ensemble techniques like bagging and boosting. By merging several weak learners into one strong learner, these methods greatly increased the prediction models' accuracy and resilience. One of the most well-known boosting algorithms, AdaBoost was created by Yoav Freund and Robert

Schapire, and it has been extensively used in many different fields.

In the 2000s, the internet's widespread use and the emergence of big data presented machine learning with both new potential and difficulties. Large-scale data collection and processing made it possible to create increasingly complex models and use machine learning to solve a wider variety of issues. During this time, there were significant improvements made in techniques like natural language processing, anomaly detection, and clustering.

The resurrection of neural networks, or "deep learning," in the late 2000s and early 2010s was one of the most revolutionary advances in the history of machine learning. Deep learning involves training multi-layer neural networks with enormous datasets using methods like convolutional neural networks (CNNs) and recurrent neural networks (RNNs), as well as advancements in computing power. Researchers like Geoffrey Hinton, Yann LeCun, and Yoshua Bengio pioneered work that showed deep learning's extraordinary powers in tasks like speech recognition, picture identification, and natural language understanding.

In several benchmarks and competitions, such as the ImageNet Large Scale Visual Recognition Challenge, deep learning models have proven they can function at a level that is comparable to human performance.As a result of significant investments made by businesses and academic organizations in deep learning research, these models have become widely used in industry and have seen tremendous developments.

Machine learning has been developing over the past several years due to ongoing study and developments in technology. Methods like reinforcement learning, which concentrate on teaching agents to interact with their surroundings and make decisions in a sequential manner, have become more and more popular. The success of AlphaGo and other AI systems that can play games is a prime example of how advances in reinforcement learning have shown that machine learning is capable of solving challenging, real-world issues.

The capabilities and uses of machine learning are expected to be further enhanced by its integration with other cutting-edge technologies, including edge computing, quantum computing, and the Internet of Things (IoT). In order to address issues about transparency, bias, and reliability, researchers are looking into approaches to improve the interpretability, fairness, and robustness of machine learning models.

Ethical considerations are now given more weight in the development and use of machine learning systems. More focus is being paid to concerns such as algorithmic bias, data privacy, and the effects of automation on society. The discipline is shifting toward more morally and responsibly conducted work, stressing the importance of openness, responsibility, and diversity in machine learning applications and research.

Looking ahead, machine learning has a tonne of promise and potential. Subsequent developments in algorithms, computing capacity, and data accessibility are anticipated to propel additional discoveries and improvements. Healthcare, banking, transportation, and education are just a few of the industries that machine learning has the potential to completely transform by providing fresh approaches to complex problems and improving human potential.

In conclusion, a number of innovative concepts, theoretical advancements, and real-world applications characterize the inception and early history of machine learning. From the first conceptions of artificial intelligence to the development of deep learning and beyond, the area of machine learning has grown to be a potent and revolutionary one. Numerous trailblazing scholars' contributions and the coming together of different fields have impacted the voyage, creating a dynamic and rich environment. With its potential to transform our world in profound and unprecedented ways and to open up new avenues for innovation, discovery, and societal influence, machine learning promises to be a game-changer.

Milestones in the development of AI and data science

Data science and artificial intelligence (AI) have come a long way, with many significant turning points that have molded the disciplines into what they are today. The main turning moments in the growth of data analysis and machine learning (AI) are examined in this section, along with their origins, significant discoveries, and the theoretical and technological advances that have powered their development.

The philosophical underpinnings of artificial intelligence (AI) date back to the ancient periods, when mathematicians and philosophers contemplated the nature of intelligence and the potential for building intelligent machines. However, the formal start of artificial intelligence as a scientific field dates to the middle of the 20th century. The 1950 publication "Computing Machinery and Intelligence" by Alan Turing was one of the first and most significant milestones. Turing developed the Turing Test, a standard for judging whether a machine is capable of intelligent conduct that is indistinguishable from human behavior, in this groundbreaking book. This study established the theoretical foundation for artificial intelligence by putting forth the central AI tenet that machines are capable of learning and adapting.

Most people agree that the Dartmouth Conference in 1956 marked the beginning of AI as a legitimate academic field. Leading scientists convened at the meeting, which was organized by Claude Shannon, Nathaniel Rochester, John McCarthy, and Marvin Minsky, to talk about the potential for building intelligent machines. It was during this meeting that the term "artificial intelligence" was first used, officially launching the discipline. The conversations and concepts we had at Dartmouth laid the groundwork for further AI research and development.

The next few years saw a sharp advancement in AI research, driven by hope and lofty objectives. Frank Rosenblatt created the perceptron, a primitive form of artificial neural network that could learn from information, in 1957. the work of Rosenblatt study was important because it showed that robots could be trained to recognize patterns and draw inferences from incoming data. This was a forerunner of the neural networks that would eventually play a key role in artificial intelligence and machine learning.

When Joseph Weizenbaum developed ELIZA, one of the first natural language processing (NLP) programs, in 1965, it was another significant turning point. ELIZA used basic pattern-matching techniques to mimic a human-computer conversation. Even though ELIZA was somewhat primary, it showed that computers could communicate with people in ways that resembled those of humans, which sparked additional interest in natural language processing and human-computer interaction.

Expert systems began to appear in the 1970s and 1980s, marking a significant development in AI. Expert systems were created to simulate human experts' decision-making processes in particular fields. Among the most prominent instances was MYCIN, made in the 1970s at Stanford University. An expert system called MYCIN was used to identify bacterial illnesses and provide remedies. It demonstrated the ability of AI to help with complex, domain-specific activities by making decisions using a knowledge base of rules compiled by medical specialists.

Despite significant advancements in AI research, the discipline also encountered difficulties and periods of inactivity known as "AI winters." During these periods, funding and interest in AI research declined, and advancements stalled. Due in part to the shortcomings of early AI systems and their inability to live up to the high standards established by their early triumphs, the first AI winter happened in the middle of the 1970s. New paradigms developed as a result of ongoing study despite these obstacles.

Machine learning emerged as a separate area of artificial intelligence in the 1980s. Developing methods that enable computers to learn from data and improve over time is the aim of machine learning. The development of the backpropagation algorithm by David Rumelhart, Geoffrey Hinton, and Ronald Williams in 1986 was a significant turning point during this time. Backpropagation made it possible to efficiently modify weights in multi-layer networks, which completely changed the training of artificial neural networks. This innovation cleared the path for the creation of more advanced neural networks by addressing many of the shortcomings of previous models.

The field of data science started to take shape at the same time. Large-scale data gathering, processing, and interpretation are all included in data science in order to derive valuable insights. The basis for contemporary data science was established in the 1980s and 1990s with the expansion of data availability and the development of computational capacity. The advent of databases and data warehousing technologies, which made it easier to store and retrieve big datasets, were two significant advancements during this time.

Both artificial intelligence (AI) and data science made tremendous strides in the 1990s and early 2000s thanks to advances in theory and real-world applications. During this period, one of the most significant developments in AI was the creation of support vector machines (SVMs) by Vladimir Vapnik and associates. SVMs are robust algorithms with solid performance and theoretical guarantees for applications involving regression and classification. They spread rapidly and were employed in many other contexts, adding to the expanding toolkit of machine learning professionals.

Another revolutionary turning point was the advent of group techniques like bagging and boosting. By merging several weak learners into one strong learner, these methods greatly increased the prediction models' accuracy and resilience. One of the most well-known boosting algorithms, AdaBoost, was created by Yoav Freund and Robert Schapire, and it has been extensively used in many different fields.

AI and data science faced new potential and difficulties in the 2000s with the development of the internet and the emergence of big data. Large-scale data collection and processing made it possible to create increasingly complex models and use AI to solve a wider range of issues. During this time, there were major improvements made in techniques like natural language processing, anomaly detection, and clustering.

The resurrection of neural networks, or deep learning, in the late 2000s and early 2010s was one of the most revolutionary advancements in AI. Using techniques like convolutional neural networks (CNNs) and recurrent neural networks (RNNs), along with advances in computer capacity, deep learning entails training multi-layer neural networks with massive datasets. Researchers like Geoffrey Hinton, Yann LeCun, and Yoshua Bengio pioneered work that showed deep learning's unique powers in tasks like speech recognition, picture identification, and natural language understanding.

Deep learning models have demonstrated their ability to perform at a level comparable to humans in a number of benchmarks and competitions, including the ImageNet Large Scale Visual Recognition Challenge. As a result of significant investments made by businesses and academic organizations in deep learning research, these models have become widely used in industry and have seen tremendous developments.

The creation of reinforcement learning, a paradigm centered on teaching agents to make successive judgments by interacting with an environment, was another critical turning point in AI and data science. The groundbreaking textbook "Reinforcement Learning: An Introduction" by Richard Sutton and Andrew Barto, published in 1998, is credited with inspiring the concept of reinforcement learning. However, the field gained prominence due to deep reinforcement learning's success, which is demonstrated by the accomplishments of AlphaGo and other AI systems that can play games. DeepMind's AlphaGo, which beat the world champion Go player in 2016, explained how AI may be used to solve challenging, practical issues.

Data science kept developing alongside AI, propelled by the creation of new tools and methods for data analysis as well as the expansion of data availability. Big data technologies like Hadoop and Spark enabled large-scale dataset processing, and advances in data visualization and exploratory data analysis made it easier to extract insightful information from data. A thriving community of practitioners and researchers was fostered by the democratization of access to data science tools and methodologies brought about by the advent of open-source software, which includes programming languages like Python and R.

As AI and data science technologies are developed and used, ethical issues are becoming more and more crucial. More focus is being paid to concerns such algorithmic bias, data privacy, and the effects of automation on society. The discipline is shifting toward more morally and responsibly conducted work, stressing the importance of openness, responsibility, and diversity in data science and artificial intelligence applications.

Notable theoretical and practical developments characterize the turning points in the development of AI and data science. Every significant growth in these domains, from the early conceptual underpinnings established by Turing and the Dartmouth Conference to the rebirth of neural networks and the emergence of big data, has aided in their evolution. There have been phases of tremendous invention and advancement in the development of AI and data science, as well as difficulties and disappointments. On the whole, nevertheless, the trajectory has been one of growing skill and sophistication.

Looking ahead, data science and artificial intelligence have a bright future ahead of them. Subsequent developments in algorithms, computing capacity, and data accessibility are anticipated to propel additional discoveries and improvements. Data science will increasingly leverage big data and sophisticated analytics to tackle difficult problems and reach meaningful conclusions, while AI research will continue to rely primarily on machine learning, deep learning, and reinforcement learning.

When AI and data science are integrated with other cutting-edge technologies like edge computing, quantum computing, and the Internet of Things (IoT), there is promise for further enhancing these technologies' capabilities and applications. In order to address concerns about transparency, bias, and reliability, researchers are looking into ways to improve the interpretability, fairness, and robustness of AI models. In order to ensure that AI and data science technologies are developed and implemented responsibly and reasonably, ethical considerations will continue to be a key area of study.

One of the most exciting aspects of the field is the potential for AI and data science to revolutionize other industries, such as healthcare, banking, transportation, and education. AI-powered diagnostic tools and tailored medicine hold promise for bettering patient outcomes and cutting costs in the healthcare industry. AI-driven algorithms in finance can improve investing strategies, risk management, and fraud detection. Autonomous cars and intelligent infrastructure have the potential to improve efficiency and safety in transportation. AI-enabled personalized learning in education can enhance student outcomes by offering customized learning experiences.

The turning points in the advancement of data science and artificial intelligence are evidence of the resourcefulness and tenacity of practitioners and researchers. Every significant development in deep learning and big data, from their early theoretical underpinnings to their most recent innovations, has aided in the growth and development of these domains. Future developments in artificial intelligence (AI) and data science have the potential to drastically and previously unheard-ofly change our environment while also creating new avenues for social impact, creativity, and discovery.

In summary, a number of turning points have changed the areas of artificial intelligence (AI) and data science into what they are today. Every significant development in these domains, from the early conceptual underpinnings established by Alan Turing and the Dartmouth Conference to the resurrection of neural networks and the emergence of big data, has aided in their evolution. There have been phases of tremendous invention and advancement in the development of AI and data science, as well as difficulties and disappointments. On the whole, nevertheless, the trajectory has been one of growing skill and sophistication.

When AI and data science are integrated with other cutting-edge technologies like edge computing, quantum computing, and the Internet of Things (IoT), there is promise for further enhancing these technologies' capabilities and applications. In order to address concerns about transparency, bias, and reliability, researchers are looking into ways to improve the interpretability, fairness, and robustness of AI models. In order to ensure that AI and data science technologies are developed and implemented responsibly and reasonably, ethical considerations will continue to be a key area of study.

Future developments in artificial intelligence (AI) and data science have the potential to drastically and previously unheard-ofly change our environment while also creating new avenues for social impact, creativity, and discovery. The turning points in the advancement of data science and artificial intelligence are evidence of the resourcefulness and tenacity of practitioners and researchers. Every significant development in deep learning and big data, from their early theoretical underpinnings to their most recent innovations, has aided in the growth and development of these domains. There is still a long way to go in the development of AI and data science, and exciting new discoveries are expected in the future.

Key figures and pioneers

Prominent individuals and trailblazers have significantly influenced the domains of artificial intelligence (AI) and data science, propelling creativity and expanding the realm of possibilities. These people have had a profound impact on the development of artificial intelligence (AI) and data science, setting the groundwork for the current breakthroughs in the fields through their groundbreaking research, imaginative concepts, and valuable contributions.

Alan Turing, who is frequently recognized as the founder of computer science and artificial intelligence, is among the most essential individuals in the history of AI. Turing's groundbreaking research brought ideas that still influence AI today and established the theoretical foundation for the discipline. In his renowned study "Computing Machinery and Intelligence," published in 1950, Alan Turing established the Turing Test as a standard to evaluate if a machine is capable of displaying intelligent behavior that is indistinguishable from human conduct. This concept posed a challenge to the accepted definition of intelligence and laid the groundwork for later AI research.

John McCarthy, who created the phrase "artificial intelligence" and arranged the Dartmouth Conference in 1956—generally recognized as the beginning of AI as a field—is another important person in the early development of AI. McCarthy's foresight and direction were crucial in creating AI as a separate academic area and a community of researchers committed to its advancement. His work set the foundation for decades of AI study and development.

Renowned AI researcher Marvin Minsky, who also co-founded the MIT AI Lab, made significant advances in the fields of neural networks, robotics, and cognitive science. Co-authored by Minsky and Seymour Papert, "Perceptrons," a 1969 book, examined the shortcomings of early neural network models and established the groundwork for upcoming developments in the subject.

Even though neural networks were initially met with suspicion, Minsky's work helped to revive interest in the field in the 1980s and 1990s, which resulted in the creation of increasingly complex models and methods.

Another well-known AI pioneer, Herbert Simon, made significant advances in cognitive psychology as well as AI. Expert systems and other AI applications have their roots in Simon's research on decision-making and problem-solving. His groundbreaking study on the process of decision-making in economic organizations earned him the 1978 Nobel Prize in Economics, highlighting the multidisciplinary character of his body of work.

Influential people have also contributed significantly to the development of data science as a field and to our understanding of how to draw conclusions and knowledge from data. John Tukey, a statistician and pioneer in exploratory data analysis, is one such person. Tukey's work offered ideas like the box plot and the rapid Fourier transform and established the groundwork for contemporary data visualization methods. His focus on using graphical analysis and visualization to interpret data transformed statistics and set the stage for further advancements in data science.

Jim Gray, a computer scientist well-known for his work on database systems and data management, is another significant person in the history of data science. The fields of data-intensive computing and cloud computing were made possible by Gray's work on distributed computing and large-scale data processing. His work on the creation of scalable and effective methods for processing and storing data has had a significant influence on how data is handled and examined in contemporary businesses.

Geoffrey Hinton, known as the "a father of firmly acquiring knowledge," has significantly advanced the science of artificial intelligence through his studies on deep learning and neural networks. Hinton's contributions to the fields of computer vision, speech recognition, and natural language processing—particularly in the areas of backpropagation, deep belief networks, and Boltzmann machines—have been essential in many recent advances in artificial intelligence. His groundbreaking work has brought him multiple honors and recognitions, including the 2018 Turing Award, and it has motivated a new wave of researchers to push the limits of artificial intelligence.

Convolutional neural networks (CNNs) and their uses in computer vision have been significantly advanced by Yann LeCun, another well-known name in the field of deep learning. Computer vision has undergone a revolution thanks to LeCun's research on CNNs and their capacity to learn hierarchical representations of visual data. This has resulted in advances in tasks like object recognition, image classification, and image segmentation. His contributions have significantly changed how we interact with and comprehend visual data, opening up new possibilities for use in anything from driverless cars to healthcare.

Numerous researchers, engineers, and practitioners have advanced AI and data science in addition to these influential individuals. The history of artificial intelligence (AI) and data science is a monument to the cooperative efforts of people across disciplines and generations, from pioneers like Claude Shannon, who established the foundations of information theory, to modern researchers pushing the boundaries of machine learning and AI.

Future generations of scholars and practitioners will be motivated to push the frontiers of data science and artificial intelligence by the lasting impact of these influential individuals and trailblazers. Their contributions serve as a reminder of the transformational power of human intellect and the potential of AI and data science to alter the future of society as we face new opportunities and challenges in the digital era.

In summary, influential people and trailblazers have significantly shaped the domains of data science and artificial intelligence, spurring creativity and expanding the realm of possibility. Decades of study and development in artificial intelligence (AI) and data science have been made possible by the efforts of visionaries such as Alan Turing, John McCarthy, and Geoffrey Hinton, as well as more recent luminaries like Yann LeCun. As we look to the future, their legacy will keep motivating researchers and practitioners to push the envelope and make use of data science and artificial intelligence's transformative potential for the benefit of society.

CHAPTER II

Understanding Data

Types of data: structured vs. unstructured

In the digital age, data is essential to decision-making, innovation, and corporate and government operations. Although it takes many different forms, organized and unstructured data are the two primary categories into which it may be divided. Leveraging the full potential of these two forms of data in analytics, machine learning, and other applications requires an understanding of their distinctions.

Information arranged according to a predetermined structure is referred to as structured data. Relational databases, which use a schema to specify the data's format, are frequently used to store this kind of data. Usually quantitative in nature, structured data consists of numbers and values that are simple to measure and evaluate. Names, addresses, phone numbers, transaction histories, and inventory counts are a few types of structured data. Because structured data is organized, it is easy to manage, search for, and analyze using SQL (Structured Query Language), which makes it an efficient querying tool.

The simplicity of the use of structured data is one of its main benefits. Structured data is relatively simple to input, save, and retrieve since it follows a precise standard. For many years, structured data has been essential to businesses and organizations' key functions, including supply chain management, customer relationship management (CRM), and financial reporting. Because structured data is predictable and consistent, it's perfect for creating dashboards, reports, and visualizations that offer insights into metrics like as key performance indicators (KPIs).

Structured data does have certain restrictions, though. Any modifications to the data structure may be time-consuming and expensive due to the rigidity of its schema. Furthermore, structured data only makes up a small portion of the information that businesses may access. Although it can capture certain kinds of data that are easily arranged into rows and columns, it frequently overlooks the wealth of information that can be found in alternative formats. Unstructured data is helpful in this situation.

As the name implies, unstructured data lacks a preset structure or format. It contains many different kinds of data, including emails, sections on social media, text, photos, videos, and audio files, among others. The nuances, context, and depth of information that organized data cannot convey are often captured by unstructured data, which is qualitative in nature. An email, for instance, contains metadata about the sender, receiver, and timestamps in addition to text. When examined, this metadata might yield insightful information.

Complexity is one of the main problems with unstructured data. Unstructured data need more complex storage options, like NoSQL databases or data lakes, in contrast to structured data, which is readily stored in relational databases. These systems offer more flexibility and scalability since they are built to manage massive volumes of various data kinds without a set structure.

Advanced methods like artificial intelligence (AI), machine learning, and natural language processing (NLP) are frequently used in the analysis of unstructured data. By removing essential patterns, trends, and insights from unstructured data, these technologies help businesses better understand their clients, marketplaces, and internal business processes. Sentiment analysis, for example, can determine the general sentiment from sections on social media, while image recognition may recognize objects and features in images and videos.

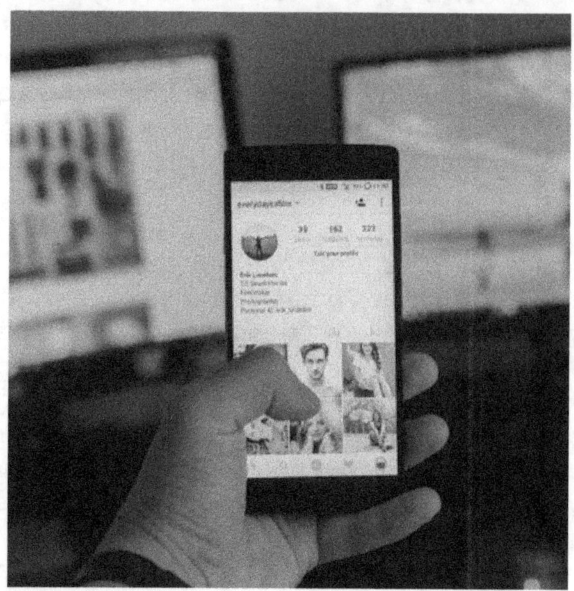

Even with its intricacy, unstructured data presents noteworthy benefits. It offers a more complete picture of reality, bringing to light context and subtleties that structured data could miss. Organizations can find hidden insights, identify new patterns, and make better decisions by studying unstructured data. In industries like marketing, where a better grasp of consumer attitude and behavior can result in more successful campaigns and plans, this kind of data is handy.

Data integration is a crucial factor to take into account when working with both organized and unstructured data. Both kinds of data are used by most businesses, and combining them can be difficult. While unstructured data can be found on a variety of platforms, including social media, cloud storage, and internal document repositories, structured data is typically found in traditional databases and corporate systems. Vital data management techniques, such as data governance, data quality, and data security, are necessary for effective data integration.

Data governance guarantees that information is handled ethically and uniformly throughout the company. It entails setting guidelines, norms, and practices for gathering, storing, and using data. Preserving the accuracy, comprehensiveness, and dependability of data is the core goal of data quality. Making wise business decisions and guaranteeing regulatory compliance requires access to high-quality data. Data security is the process of shielding information from dangers, breaches, and unwanted access. Robust data governance and security protocols are becoming increasingly necessary as the amount and diversity of data increase.

Data storage is a crucial component in managing both organized and unstructured data. Relational databases, which work effectively with tabular data with a set schema, are where structured data is usually kept. These databases facilitate quick data retrieval and searching through the use of indexing and other optimization techniques. Relational database management systems (RDBMS) are exemplified by Oracle, PostgreSQL, and MySQL.

Conversely, unstructured data frequently calls for more adaptable storage options. Large amounts of data and a variety of data types can be handled by NoSQL databases like MongoDB, Cassandra, and Elasticsearch. For some use scenarios, they are more performant and scalable than regular RDBMS. A concentrated location for extensive data analytics is offered by data lakes, which have the capacity to hold unstructured, semi-structured, and structured data together. To construct data lakes, technologies like Amazon S3 and Apache Hadoop are frequently employed.

There are also notable differences in the handling and examination of organized and unstructured data. Conventional tools and methodologies for business intelligence (BI) analysis can be used to structure data. These tools offer data visualization, reporting, and querying capabilities. They work well at creating scorecards, dashboards, and other kinds of visualizations that support data-driven decision-making and performance monitoring for businesses.

However, unstructured data analysis frequently calls for more sophisticated techniques. Text data can be processed and analyzed by NLP approaches, which can also extract sentiment, keywords, and topic information. Tasks involving categorization and predictive analytics are made possible by machine learning algorithms' ability to find patterns and relationships in unstructured data. Image identification, speech-to-text conversion, and video analysis are made possible by AI technologies like deep learning, which can do intricate analyses on photos, videos, and audio recordings.

New platforms and tools that can manage both structured and unstructured data have been developed as a result of the convergence of these data analysis fields. Organizations are able to combine and analyze both structured and unstructured data together thanks to these integrated analytics platforms, which offer a single picture of the data. They will be able to comprehend their operations and surroundings more thoroughly and with more profound insights if they take this action.

The explosion of digital material and the rise of social media are two significant factors contributing to the growing significance of unstructured data. Social networking sites like Facebook, Twitter, and Instagram are used by billions of people, which results in the daily generation of enormous amounts of unstructured data. This data, which comes in the form of text, photos, videos, and other material, provides insightful information on the trends, preferences, and behavior of consumers. Businesses are using this data to better client engagement, expand their marketing campaigns, and create new goods and services.

Similarly, the growth of IoT (Internet of Things) devices has led to an explosion of unstructured data. Sensors, wearable technology, and smart appliances are examples of Internet of Things devices that continuously provide streams of data in different formats. Real-time insights into operations may be obtained from this data, which can help with supply chain optimization, predictive maintenance, and improving customer experiences.

Another sector where unstructured data is growing more and more significant is healthcare. Unstructured data in healthcare includes information found in clinical notes, imaging results, genetic data, and medical records. Advanced medical research, tailored treatments, and better patient outcomes are all possible benefits of this data analysis. For example, NLP can parse clinical notes to extract critical medical information, while AI algorithms can analyze medical photos to detect diseases early.

Structured data is still necessary even though unstructured data is becoming more and more important. The foundation of many corporate operations and decision-making procedures is provided by structured data. It is frequently utilized for transactional tasks like order processing, inventory control, and money handling. Because of its consistency and dependability, structured data is a reliable source for essential business operations.

To sum up, both structured and unstructured data are essential components of the contemporary data environment. Because of its standardized and ordered style, structured data is handy for traditional business operations and decision-making. It is a mainstay in many industries due to its simplicity of use and compatibility with relational databases. Unstructured data, on the other hand, provides a more thorough understanding of reality due to its rich and varied character. Thanks to the development of artificial intelligence, machine learning, and natural language processing (NLP), organizations may now make more strategic and informed decisions.

The capacity to efficiently handle, integrate, and analyze both structured and unstructured data will be a critical differentiator for businesses as the amount and variety of data continue to rise. In the digital age, those who can leverage the power of both forms of data will have an advantage in terms of innovation, competitiveness, and overall success. To maximize the value of data and produce positive results, it will be crucial to strike a balance between the usage of structured and unstructured data while maintaining robust data governance, quality, and security.

Data collection methods

In many industries where information is used to make decisions, including business and research, gathering data is an essential step in the process. The techniques used to obtain data can have a significant impact on the validity, correctness, and dependability of the information received. There are several ways to gather data, and each one works well for a particular set of goals, situations, and research questions. It is crucial to comprehend these techniques, as well as the benefits and drawbacks of each, in order to choose the best course of action for a specific circumstance.

The survey is one of the most basic ways to gather data.

Questionnaires are usually used in surveys to collect data from a large number of respondents. There are several ways to conduct these questionnaires: online, via mail, via phone, or in person. Because of their versatility, surveys can be used to collect data that is both quantitative and qualitative. They are beneficial for gathering information on demographic traits, attitudes, beliefs, and behaviors. The surveys' organized format makes it simple to analyze and compare replies. However, elements like question design, response rates, and respondent honesty can have an impact on how accurate survey data is.

Interviews are yet another popular technique for gathering data. During an interview, the respondent and the researcher speak with each other directly and one-on-one. Depending on the intended degree of flexibility, they might be unstructured, semi-structured, or structured. A predetermined list of questions is used in structured interviews to guarantee uniformity throughout the process. Semi-structured interviews provide the researcher with some leeway to delve further into subjects. In unstructured interviews, the interviewer is free to follow the respondent's lead and probe more freely, resulting in a more conversational exchange. When gathering comprehensive, in-depth knowledge and comprehending intricate behaviors, motivations, and experiences, interviews are constructive. They may take a lot of time and lead to interviewer bias.

Focus groups are an additional technique for gathering qualitative data in which a moderator leads a small group of participants in a discussion on a particular subject. This approach is helpful in examining beliefs, attitudes, and concepts in a social setting. Group interactions can produce a wealth of information and highlight insights that may not surface in one-on-one interviews. In social science, health, and market research, focus groups are frequently employed. However, group dynamics, such as influential participants overshadowing quieter ones, might affect the data gathered from focus groups. Furthermore, it isn't easy to extrapolate the findings to a broader population.

A method of gathering data called observation entails methodically documenting actions, occasions, or circumstances as they transpire in their natural environments. There are two types of this method: participant and non-participant. In contrast to non-participant observation, which keeps the researcher impartial, participant observation involves the researcher joining the group being observed. When examining behaviors and interactions in real-time, observation is beneficial as it offers a degree of context and information that other approaches can miss. But it can also be arbitrary and affected by the presence of the observer, which could change the way the people being watched behave.

In experiments, one or more variables are changed to see how they affect a dependent variable. This is a quantitative data collecting technique. Scientific research frequently uses this technique to test hypotheses and identify cause-and-effect linkages. Experiments can be carried out in natural settings or in controlled conditions like labs. Experiments have the primary benefit of being able to control and isolate factors, which yields compelling proof of causation. They may be challenging to develop and lose their external validity if the experimental settings are not very similar to actual circumstances.

Utilizing secondary data or already existing records is another quantitative approach. This entails reviewing information that has already been gathered by others, including records kept by organizations and government agencies and surveys that have already been completed. In addition to saving time and money, using existing records gives you access to massive, thorough datasets. However, as the data was not gathered with their particular study topics in mind, researchers need to exercise caution regarding its quality and applicability. Furthermore, there can be restrictions on the applications and interpretations of the data.

With the development of digital technology, online data collection has grown in popularity. Web scraping, social media analysis, and online surveys fall under this category. Web surveys are a popular option for many researchers since they may swiftly and affordably reach a large audience. In order to research trends, attitudes, and behaviors, social media analysis entails extracting data from websites like Facebook, Twitter, and Instagram. Using software to retrieve data from websites automatically is known as web scraping. Access to vast, varied datasets and real-time data is one benefit of online data collection. It also brings up questions regarding sample representativeness, ethical issues, and data privacy.

A case study is a comprehensive data collection technique that entails a close analysis of one or a small group of people. This approach is frequently used to investigate complicated problems and give a complete grasp of the context in the social sciences, business, and education. Case studies can make use of a range of data collection techniques, such as document analysis, interviews, and observation. They are helpful in producing in-depth, contextualized knowledge and fostering a thorough comprehension of the subject. Case study results, however, are difficult to extrapolate to a broader population.

Another type of data collection that involves gathering information from the same people over an extended period of time is longitudinal investigations. This approach is beneficial for researching alterations and advancements throughout time. Studies using a longitudinal design can yield important information about patterns, causal connections, and the long-term consequences of interventions. However, they take a lot of time and money, and researchers have to be ready to handle problems like participant attrition and shifting study conditions.

A qualitative approach to gathering data, ethnography entails studying people and cultures in their own habitats. Long stretches of time are spent by ethnographers observing and engaging with the community or group they are researching, frequently taking part in its regular activities. This approach offers a comprehensive, in-depth comprehension of cultural practices and social phenomena. For the purpose of examining intricate social concerns, actions, and meanings, ethnography is especially helpful. It takes a lot of effort, though, and the researcher's viewpoint and interpretation have a significant impact on the results.

Researchers now have access to a broader variety of techniques thanks to the usage of technology in data collection. Mobile data collection is the process of acquiring data using cellphones, tablets, and other mobile devices. Surveys, GPS tracking, and real-time data entering are a few examples of this. Respondents in rural or difficult-to-reach places can be reached by mobile data gathering, which is effective. It also makes real-time data collecting possible, which improves the timeliness and accuracy of the information acquired. However, it needs a technical infrastructure and is susceptible to problems with connectivity, battery life, and device compatibility.

Two examples of wearable technology, which is another novel approach to data collection, are smartwatches and fitness trackers. Heart rate, level of physical activity, sleep patterns, and other physiological and behavioral factors can all be continuously monitored and recorded by these devices. Numerous objective, real-time data points from wearable technology are available for use in behavioral study, health research, and personalized treatment. To protect privacy and security, wearable device data must be appropriately maintained, and the devices' correctness and dependability must be confirmed.

Crowdsourcing is a technique for collecting data that entails obtaining data from a sizable, geographically dispersed population, sometimes using internet platforms. Through the use of a varied group's aggregate knowledge and talents, this method collects data rapidly and effectively. There are several uses for crowdsourcing, including content creation, problem-solving, and data labeling. It has the benefit of providing access to a variety of viewpoints and levels of experience. However, organizing and validating the contributions can be difficult, and the data quality can vary.

Another cutting-edge technique for gathering data is sensor technology, which makes use of sensors to identify and quantify physical processes. Sensors can collect information about human activity and behavior as well as environmental factors like temperature, humidity, and air quality. In industries including smart cities, healthcare, and environmental monitoring, sensor data is frequently used. It offers continuous, unbiased data that is useful for monitoring and analyzing in real time. Sensor network deployment and upkeep can be expensive, and the data collected needs to be appropriately calibrated and verified.

Biometric data collection is the process of gathering information by biological and physiological measures, such as iris scans, fingerprints, and facial recognition. This technique is frequently applied in identification and security applications as well as in medical research. Biometric data is helpful for many reasons because it gives precise and distinct information about individuals. However, it brings up serious ethical and privacy issues; thus, in order to safeguard people's rights and freedoms, biometric data use needs to be adequately controlled and regulated.

Using satellite or aerial photography, remote sensing is a technique for gathering data on the surface of the Earth.

Urban planning, forestry, agriculture, and environmental monitoring are among the industries that frequently use this technique. Comprehensive, large-scale data from remote sensing can be utilized to examine vegetation, water resources, land use, and other environmental aspects. Its benefit is that it can cover large areas and provide data that is hard or impossible to gather on the ground. However, the data can be impacted by variables like weather and sensor resolution, and the interpretation of remote sensing data necessitates specific knowledge and equipment.

The choice of approach relies on the goals of the study, the type of data required, and the study's environment. Each of these data collection techniques has advantages and disadvantages of its own. To strengthen the validity and dependability of their data and to triangulate their conclusions, researchers frequently employ a variety of techniques. For instance, research on consumer behavior might use social media analysis to track trends and sentiments in real-time, interviews to obtain in-depth insights into motivations and attitudes, and surveys to gather quantitative data on purchase patterns.

In summary, data collecting is a comprehensive and intricate procedure that is necessary to obtain correct and trustworthy information. The research questions, the type of data required, the resources available, and the study's setting all influence the choice of data-gathering method. Researchers can choose the best data gathering strategy for their unique requirements by being aware of the benefits and drawbacks of various techniques. The objective is to gather data that is precise, dependable, and pertinent in order to support informed decision-making and advance knowledge across a range of sectors. This can be achieved through the use of sophisticated technology, such as mobile devices and sensors, or more conventional techniques, such as surveys and interviews.

Data storage and management

Data management and storage are now essential elements for individuals, companies, and governments operating in the digital era. The Internet, mobile devices, social media, and the Internet of Things (IoT) have all contributed to the exponential rise of data, which makes it necessary to have reliable, effective, and secure ways to store and manage this enormous amount of data. Data that is appropriately managed and stored is available for analysis and decision-making, as well as being dependable, secure, and accessible. The several facets of data administration and storage are examined in this section, along with data management techniques, obstacles, and emerging trends.

Digital information must be stored so that it may be retrieved and used when needed. This process is known as data storage. Data was traditionally kept on a tangible medium like disks, tapes, and paper. Nonetheless, digital techniques are primarily used in contemporary data storage systems. The hard disk drive is one of the most commonly utilized forms of digital information storage (HDD). For a long time, HDDs have been the industry standard because they provide high storage capacity at affordable prices. On rotating platters, they encode data magnetically. Though widely used, HDDs have drawbacks, including slower data recovery speeds than newer technologies and physical damage susceptibility.

The development of solid-state drives, or SSDs, has significantly advanced data storage technology. SSDs store data on flash memory, which is faster and more reliable than HDDs because it doesn't have any moving parts. SSDs are more costly per gigabyte than HDDs, but they provide faster data access times, less power usage, and more excellent reliability. SSDs are becoming more common in both consumer and business storage solutions as their cost continues to drop.

The way data is managed and kept has been completely transformed by cloud storage. It makes it possible to store data on distant servers that can be accessed online. Scalable storage options that can handle different volumes of data are provided by cloud storage providers like Microsoft Azure, Google Cloud Platform, and Amazon Web Services (AWS). Cost-effectiveness, scalability, and accessibility are just a few advantages of cloud storage. Companies may lower expenses related to maintaining physical storage infrastructure, access data from any location with an internet connection, and scale their storage needs up or down based on demand. Cloud storage does, however, also bring up issues with privacy, data security, and reliance on service providers.

Other crucial data storage options, especially for business settings, include Network Attached Storage (NAS) and Storage Area Networks (SAN). A network-attached storage device (NAS) is a specialized file storage device that facilitates data sharing and access for several users and devices. Because NAS is so simple to set up and maintain, small and medium-sized enterprises can benefit from using it. In contrast, SAN is a high-speed network that links servers and storage devices. Large companies and data centers are among the settings for which SAN is intended: these are the places where massive, high-performance storage is needed. Block-level storage is one of its features, making it perfect for applications that require dependable, quick access to significant amounts of data.

The techniques, procedures, and technological tools used to manage data at every stage of its lifecycle—from production and storage to retrieval and deletion—are collectively referred to as data management. Proper data management guarantees that information is precise, dependable, safe, and observable. Data governance is a crucial aspect of data management that entails the establishment of guidelines, protocols, and standards for data administration. Data governance guarantees that, throughout the organization, data is treated consistently and legally. Data quality, data privacy, data security, and data lifecycle management are some of its components.

An essential component of data management is data quality. Data of the highest caliber is fast, accurate, comprehensive, and consistent. Inaccurate analysis, poor decision-making, and operational inefficiencies can result from poor data quality. Organizations use data cleansing and validation procedures to guarantee data quality. Finding and fixing problems like duplicates, inconsistencies, and inaccuracies is known as data cleansing. Data validation ensures that the data is appropriate for its intended purpose and satisfies predetermined standards. Over time, regular data audits and monitoring aid in maintaining data quality.

Another essential element of data management is data security. Data breaches and cyberthreats have increased, making it more crucial than ever to protect sensitive data. Putting safeguards in place to stop illegal access, disclosure, change, or destruction of data is known as data security. This covers both technological and physical security measures, such as firewalls, access controls, and encryption, as well as secure data centers. Data is safeguarded through encryption, which transforms it into an unintelligible format that can only be unlocked with the correct key. Access restrictions guarantee that data can only be accessed or modified by authorized people. Firewalls monitor and regulate data entering and leaving networks, serving as a barrier between reliable and unreliable networks.

Data security and privacy are closely associated since data privacy entails safeguarding personal information about persons.Organizations must make sure that their handling of personal data conforms with legal standards in light of norms such as the Consumer Privacy Act of California (CCPA) and the Global Data Protection Regulation (GDPR). This entails getting permission before collecting data, being open and honest about how it's used, and protecting people's rights to see, amend, or remove their data. By eliminating or hiding identifying information, data anonymization, and pseudonymization procedures can contribute to privacy protection.

The practice of managing data from its creation to its ultimate disposal is known as data lifecycle management or DLM. DLM entails establishing guidelines and practices for data erasure, archiving, and retention. Retention policies outline the duration for which data must be retained in accordance with business, legal, and regulatory needs. Moving inactive data to long-term storage for compliance or future reference is known as archiving. When data is no longer required, deletion guarantees that it is safely and permanently erased. With the use of efficient DLM, organizations may reduce the risk of data breaches, save storage costs, and adhere to regulations.

Structured data management requires the use of database management systems (DBMS). Software that provides an interface for working with databases and enables users to add, update, remove, and create data is known as a database management system (DBMS). DBMSs come in different flavors, such as relational, NoSQL, and in-memory databases. Database management systems (RDBMS) such as the following platforms: MySQL and the Oracle manage data in tables with specific relationships using structured query language (SQL). RDBMSs work effectively with transactional applications that need integrity and consistency.

MongoDB, Cassandra, and Couchbase are examples of NoSQL databases that are made to manage unstructured and semi-structured data. Big data and real-time web applications can benefit from their high performance, flexible schemas, and horizontal scalability. Document, key-value, column-family, and graph databases are among the different types of NoSQL databases that are available, each suited to particular use cases and data types. Redis and Memcached are two examples of in-memory databases that store data in the system's memory rather than on disk, enabling rapid read and write operations. They are frequently employed in applications that need low-latency data access, real-time analytics, and caching.

Another crucial component of data management is data warehousing. Large amounts of organized data from various sources are centralized and kept in data warehouses. Rather than being used for transaction processing, it is intended for inquiry and analysis. With data warehouses, businesses can execute sophisticated queries, combine data from disparate operational systems, and create reports and dashboards for business intelligence (BI) and decision-making. The process of taking data from source systems, altering it to ensure consistency and quality, and then loading it into the warehouse is known as data extraction, transformation, and loading (ETL) in data warehousing.

To manage the enormous amounts, diversity, and velocity of data generated in today's digital world, big data solutions have evolved. Two well-known big data frameworks are Apache Hadoop and Apache Spark. Across computer clusters, Hadoop's distributed processing and storage technology makes it possible to analyze enormous datasets. MapReduce is used for processing, whereas the Hadoop Distributed File System (HDFS) is used for storage. In contrast to Hadoop, Spark is an in-memory processing platform that provides faster data processing capabilities. Machine learning, real-time streaming, batch processing, and other data processing tasks are supported.

Integrating data from several sources to present a cohesive picture is known as data integration, and it is an essential component of data management. Because data formats, schemas, and semantics are heterogeneous, data integration can be complex. These issues are addressed by methods and tools, including data federation, virtualization, and ETL. Data is extracted from source systems using ETL processes, which then alter the data to guarantee consistency and quality before loading it into a target system like a data warehouse. Through a virtual layer, data virtualization offers a unified perspective by enabling users to access and query data from many sources without physically relocating the data. Data federation aggregates information from various sources, frequently in real-time, to create a cohesive dataset.

Another crucial component of data management is metadata management. Data about data, or metadata, offers details on the data's usage, format, structure, and place of origin. To make sure that data is properly documented and accessible, metadata management entails the creation, archiving, and upkeep of metadata. Good metadata management enhances data quality, usability, and governance. It makes it possible for users to comprehend the history and context of the data, which improves data analysis, integration, and decision-making.

Two important uses of data management are business intelligence (BI) and data analytics. Data analytics is the process of analyzing data and drawing conclusions through the application of computer, statistical, and mathematical methods. BI includes all of the methods and instruments needed to convert unprocessed data into information that can be used immediately, like dashboards, reports, and visualizations. Businesses can utilize business intelligence (BI) and data analytics to identify trends, patterns, and anomalies in order to make data-driven decisions and plan their strategic initiatives. Prescriptive and predictive analytics are made possible by advanced analytics techniques like artificial intelligence (AI) and machine learning, which further improve the capacity to extract insights from data.

Disaster recovery and data backup are essential elements of data management. Making copies of data is known as data backup, and it serves as insurance against data loss brought on by software bugs, hardware malfunctions, or other disturbances. Backups can be kept on a variety of media, including tape, cloud storage, and external devices. Maintaining regular backups guarantees data restoration in the event of data loss or corruption. Disaster recovery is the process of organizing and putting into action plans to restore data and carry on with business as usual after a significant disruption, including a system failure, cyberattack, or natural disaster. To maintain business continuity, disaster recovery plans usually incorporate failover, replication, and data backup features.

Addressing moral and legal issues around the use of data is another aspect of data management. Businesses need to make sure that their data practices abide by all applicable laws and rules, including HIPAA, CCPA, and GDPR. This entails getting the proper permission before collecting data, protecting data security and privacy, and being open and honest about how data is used. Ethical concerns include responsible data use and refraining from actions that can endanger people or society as a whole. Companies have to strike a balance between the advantages of data-driven innovation and the need to uphold public confidence and defend individual rights.

Future developments in data handling are being shaped by new trends in data management and storage. Edge computing is one such trend that focuses on processing data closer to its source instead of depending on centralized data centers. In order to facilitate real-time processing and decision-making for applications like the Internet of Things, driverless cars, and intelligent cities, edge computing lowers latency and bandwidth consumption. Another trend is the expanding use of artificial intelligence (AI) and machine learning in data management tasks like data integration, cleaning, and anomaly detection. Processes can be automated and optimized with AI-driven data management, increasing accuracy and efficiency.

Interest is also being generated by blockchain technology's potential in data management. An unchangeable, decentralized ledger made possible by blockchain technology can enhance data security, openness, and trust. It is beneficial for applications like supply chain management, financial transactions, and identity verification that need safe, unchangeable data. Blockchain technology is still developing, though, and there are difficulties integrating it with current data management systems.

Another cutting-edge technology that has the potential to change data management and storage completely is quantum computing. The concepts of quantum mechanics are used by quantum computers to execute complicated calculations at previously unheard-of speeds. Although quantum computing is still in its experimental stages, it has the potential to solve issues like large-scale data processing and cryptographic method optimization that are now unsolvable for classical computers.

To sum up, data management and storage are essential elements of the contemporary information environment. Organizations must implement efficient storage strategies and management techniques to keep up with the constant development of data in order to guarantee that it is valuable, dependable, safe, and accessible. The alternatives for keeping data are numerous and constantly changing, ranging from conventional storage techniques like HDDs and SSDs to cutting-edge technologies like cloud storage, NAS, SAN, and big data frameworks. Data governance, quality, security, privacy, lifecycle management, integration, metadata management, analytics, and disaster recovery are just a few of the techniques that make up effective data management. The way data is managed and kept will change even more as cutting-edge technologies like edge computing, AI, blockchain, and quantum computing advance, opening up new possibilities and solving current problems.

Data preprocessing techniques

A vital stage in the data analysis process, data preparation makes sure that the data is clean, consistent, and prepared for modeling and analysis. Preprocessing has become essential in today's environment as data is generated at an unprecedented rate from a variety of sources in order to transform raw data into a form that can be used and understood. This section explores the many data preparation strategies, examining the methodologies, relevance, and difficulties of each technique.

Data cleansing is a fundamental method in data preprocessing. Errors, inconsistencies, and missing numbers are expected in raw data, which can skew analysis and produce false conclusions. Finding and fixing these problems is the process of data cleaning, which raises the caliber of the data. Missing data is a frequent problem that can occur for a number of reasons, including human error, system malfunctions, or data corruption.

There are several approaches to deal with missing data, including replacement, imputation, and deletion. When there is little to no missing data, deletion—which is deleting entries with missing values—can be helpful. If there is a significant amount of missing data, though, it may result in the loss of important information. Using statistical techniques or algorithms like mean, median, or mode replacement, or more complex methods like regression imputation or machine learning models that forecast missing values based on other available data, is the process of imputed data filling in the gaps.

Finding and fixing outliers—data points that substantially differ from the rest of the dataset—is another aspect of data cleaning. Measurement flaws, data input problems, or actual data variability can all lead to outliers. Because outliers have the potential to distort statistical analyses and impair the effectiveness of machine learning models, it is imperative to identify them. Statistical techniques like z-scores and interquartile ranges, as well as machine learning strategies like clustering and anomaly detection algorithms, are employed in outlier detection techniques. Depending on the type of data and the goals of the research, outliers can be dealt with by removal, transformation, or capping after they have been identified.

Transforming data into a format appropriate for analysis is known as data transformation, and it is a crucial component of data preprocessing. This can involve scaling, encoding categorical variables, normalization, and standards. The act of normalizing data involves shifting its scale to lie into a predetermined range, usually between 0 and 1. This guarantees that every feature contributes equally to the analysis, which is crucial for machine learning methods that depend on distance computations, including clustering algorithms and k-nearest neighbors. In contrast, rescaling the data to have a zero mean and one standard deviation is what standardization entails. This method is beneficial for principal component analysis and linear regression, two procedures that usually presume distributed data.

Before being employed in analysis or machine learning models, categorical data—which is made up of discrete values like labels or categories—often needs to be converted into a numerical representation. One popular method for doing this is one-hot encoding, which generates binary columns for every category, each of which indicates whether the category is present in the data or not. Another method is label encoding, which gives every category a distinct integer. Label encoding introduces ordinal relationships between categories, which may not be acceptable for some types of data, although being more memory-efficient. The study's precise needs and the data's properties will determine which encoding method is best.

The most critical phases in data preprocessing are feature extraction and selection, which entail determining which characteristics or variables are most pertinent for analysis. Analyzing high-dimensional data can be difficult, and it might cause machine learning models to overfit. The practice of creating new features by merging or mathematically altering preexisting ones is known as feature extraction. To extract important aspects from textual data, for instance, text analysis techniques like word embeddings and term frequency-inverse document frequency (TF-IDF) can be applied. Selecting a subset of the most significant characteristics from the original dataset is known as feature selection. Statistical techniques like mutual information and correlation analysis, as well as more sophisticated ones like recursive feature reduction and regularization methods like Lasso and Ridge regression, can be used for this. Reducing the features enhances interpretability and model performance while also simplifying the analysis.

Another crucial preprocessing method is data integration, which is particularly useful in situations where data is gathered from several sources. Integrating data into a single, cohesive dataset from several files, databases, or streams is known as integration. Because of variations in data formats, structures, and meanings, this process can be complicated. Entity resolution, data fusion, and schema matching are examples of data integration approaches. Schema matching is the process of aligning the schemas of various datasets to guarantee accurate matching of relevant fields. Through the process of data fusion, redundant and conflicting data from several sources are combined to produce a single, cohesive dataset. To ensure consistency and completeness, entity resolution finds and merges entries that refer to the same entity across various datasets.

Techniques for data reduction are used to lower the amount of data while maintaining its essential qualities. This is especially crucial when dealing with extensive data since the volume of information can make processing, analysis, and storage complex. Techniques like dimensionality reduction, aggregation, and sampling can be used to reduce data. Selecting a representative group of data for analysis is known as sampling, and it can reduce computational requirements and speed up processing times. Through projection the data into a space with fewer dimensions, dimensionality reduction techniques like principal component analysis (PCA) and t-distributed stochastic neighbor embed (t-SNE) reduce the number of characteristics in the data while maintaining its key patterns and structures. By summarizing the data at a higher level—by calculating totals or averages, for example—aggregation helps streamline the study and draw attention to broad trends.

Techniques for converting continuous data into discrete categories or bins include data discretization and binning. To simplify the analysis and lessen the effect of noise in the data, discretization is the process of splitting the range of continuous values into a defined number of intervals. One particular kind of discretization called binding is the process of organizing continuous variables into intervals or bins. A variety of techniques exist for binning, such as equal-frequency binning, in which every bin has an equal number of observations, and equal-width binning, in which the range of values is split into bins of the same size. Data correlations and patterns that might not be visible in the continuous form can be found with the use of binning.

Another crucial component of data preprocessing is handling imbalanced data, especially when dealing with classification issues where one class is noticeably underrepresented in comparison to others. Unbalanced data can lead to biased models that perform well on the majority class but badly on the minority class. Strategies to deal with imbalanced data include resampling techniques (oversampling the minority class or undersampling the majority class) and synthetic data production techniques (Synthetic Minority Over-sampling Technique, or SMOTE). Furthermore, distinct misclassification penalties can be assigned to various classes using cost-sensitive learning techniques, which incentivizes the model to focus more on the minority class.

A standard method in machine learning, especially in domains like computer vision and natural language processing, is data augmentation, which creates an artificially larger training dataset. To do this, modified representations of the original data points are made using techniques like translations, rotations, and noise addition for images or paraphrase and synonym replacement for text. By providing a more extensive range of instances and variations, data augmentation enhances the robustness and generalization of machine learning models.

Time series data, which is made up of observations taken at particular intervals of time, has specific requirements and distinct preprocessing methods. Preprocessing time series includes generating lagged features, detecting and correcting trends and seasonality, and handling missing information. Interpolation techniques, such as spline interpolation or linear interpolation, which estimate missing values based on nearby observations, can be used to address missing values in time series data. In order to concentrate on the underlying signal, seasonality, and trend detection entail locating and eliminating long-term trends and periodic patterns from the data. In order to capture temporal dependencies in the data, lagged features are created by creating additional features that represent earlier time steps.

Another specific subset of data pretreatment is text reprocessing, which is especially important for jobs involving natural language processing (NLP). Because text data is naturally unstructured, it needs to go through a number of preparation stages before it can be put into an analysis-ready format. Tokenization, vectorization, lemmatization, stemming, and stop-word removal are examples of standard text preprocessing techniques. Tokenization is the process of dividing the text into discrete words, or tokens, which serve as the fundamental analytical units. Stop-word elimination removes terms like "and," "the," and "is," which are frequently used but convey little information. Lemmatization maps words to their base or dictionary forms, whereas stemming reduces words to their root forms by deleting suffixes. Text can be converted by vectorization into numerical representations that can be fed into machine learning models, such as TF-IDF vectors or word embeddings.

Specialized preprocessing methods are also needed for graph data, which is made up of nodes and edges that indicate relationships between entities. Graph normalization, which makes sure the graph is formatted consistently, and feature extraction, which creates node or edge features based on the graph's structure, are examples of tasks that are included in graph preprocessing. Numerical representations of nodes or complete graphs can be made using methods like node embedding and graph convolutional networks (GCNs). These representations can then be utilized for tasks like node classification, link prediction, and graph classification.

Preprocessing data has its challenges. Making sure that the preprocessing methods don't add bias or change the data in ways that compromise the analysis's validity is one of the main concerns. For instance, incorrect handling of outliers or missing data might produce biased findings, and overfitting can happen if preprocessing methods are too closely matched to the training set. Scalability is another issue, especially when working with big datasets that demand a lot of processing power. Big data preparation jobs frequently require practical algorithms and parallel processing techniques.

Data preparation entails not only technological difficulties but also moral and legal issues. It is imperative to guarantee data privacy and adherence to laws like the General Data Protection Regulation (GDPR), especially when handling sensitive personal data. By eliminating or hiding identifying information, methods like data anonymization and pseudonymization can contribute to privacy protection. Accountability and transparency are essential to guaranteeing the ethical and appropriate preparation of data.

Data preparation is expected to be influenced by machine learning and technological advancements in the future. Research is now being done in the domain of automated data preparation, where algorithms choose and apply the best preprocessing approaches automatically. Because autoML platforms automate all stages of the machine learning process, including data pretreatment, they are becoming more and more popular. By lowering the time and skill needed to prepare data and create machine learning models, these platforms can significantly increase the accessibility of data analysis for non-experts.

CHAPTER III

Statistical Foundations

Descriptive statistics

A key component of statistical analysis is descriptive statistics, which act as the foundation for more sophisticated statistical methods. It includes a variety of techniques for enumerating and characterizing the critical elements of data. Descriptive statistics concentrate on giving a clear and succinct explanation of the available data, in contrast to inferential statistics, which seeks to draw conclusions or predictions about a population from a sample. This section explores the several elements and methods of descriptive statistics, their significance, and their applications in various domains.

Measures of central tendency, which characterize the middle or typical value of a dataset, are the foundation of descriptive statistics. The three main ways to measure central tendency are the mean, median, and mode. Summing up all of the data points and dividing by the total number of points yields the mean, often known as the arithmetic average. Although it offers a clear summary of the data, skewed distributions, and outliers may have an impact. A more reliable indicator of central tendency in the presence of outliers or non-normal distributions is the median, which is the middle value obtained by sorting the data points. For categorical data, the mode—the value that appears the most frequently in the dataset—is beneficial since it indicates the most prevalent category.

The measure of variability or dispersion, which quantifies the spread or dispersion of data points about the central tendency, is another essential component of descriptive statistics. The three primary measurements of variability are variance, standard deviation, and range. Although it can be susceptible to outliers, the range—the gap between the maximum and minimum values—offers a straightforward dispersion indicator. Variance provides a more thorough evaluation of variability by calculating the average squared deviation of each data point from the mean. However, variance might be challenging to read because it is expressed in squared units. Because it is described in the same units as the data, the standard deviation—the square root of the variance—is more straightforward to understand and is frequently employed in statistical analysis.

Descriptive statistics encompass not just central tendency and variability, but also measures of shape that characterize the shape of the distribution. The two main ways to measure shape are skewness and kurtosis. The asymmetry of the data distribution is quantified by skewness. A distribution with a long right tail is indicated by a positive skew, whereas a distribution with a long left tail is shown by a negative skew. The "tailedness" of the distribution is measured by kurtosis, where a high value denotes heavy tails and a sharp peak, while a low value denotes light tails and a flatter peak.

The use of graphical representations to summarize and visualize data is also included in descriptive statistics. An intuitive grasp of data distribution, trends, and patterns can be obtained through the use of graphs and charts. Scatter plots, box plots, bar charts, and histograms are examples of common graphical approaches. A dataset's frequency distribution is displayed using a histogram, which illustrates how data points are dispersed over various bins or intervals. Bar charts show the frequency or proportion of categories and are mainly used for categorical data. The data's central tendency, variability, and outliers are visually summarized by box plots, often known as box-and-whisker plots. To investigate correlations and relationships between variables, scatter plots are utilized, wherein two variables are plotted against each other.

Descriptive statistics are used in many different fields and disciplines, such as business, economics, social sciences, and healthcare. Descriptive statistics are used in industry to examine market trends, client behavior, and sales data. To summarize monthly sales data, spot seasonal trends, and evaluate the success of marketing efforts, for instance, a business may employ measures of central tendency and variability. Descriptive statistics are used in economics to examine economic indices like GDP, unemployment, and inflation rates. These figures are used by researchers and policymakers to comprehend the state of the economy, spot patterns, and come to wise conclusions.

Descriptive statistics are essential for describing survey data, experimental findings, and observational study data in the social sciences. Measures of central tendency and variability are used by researchers to characterize the age, income, education, and health status of the study populations. Relationships between variables, such asas income and education level or the distribution of health outcomes among various demographic groups, can be seen more clearly with graphic tools. Additionally helpful in spotting patterns and trends in social phenomena, including crime rates, voting patterns, and public opinion, are descriptive statistics.

Descriptive statistics are critical to the analysis of patient data, clinical trial outcomes, and public health trends in the healthcare industry. Medical practitioners use these data to assemble patient characteristics like age, gender, and medical history, as well as clinical outcomes like treatment success rates and adverse event frequencies. Descriptive statistics are useful for monitoring the spread of infectious illnesses, determining disease risk factors, and evaluating the effectiveness of treatments and policies.

Descriptive statistics' capacity to provide data in an understandable and succinct manner that facilitates interpretation is one of its main advantages. It's crucial to understand the limitations of descriptive statistics, though. They don't permit extra-dataset generalizations or forecasts, despite offering insightful information about the data. While descriptive statistics highlight the features of the data, they do not reveal the underlying causes or workings of the systems. To make inferences about the population from a sample, inferential statistics and hypothesis testing are required.

Notwithstanding these drawbacks, descriptive statistics remain a vital instrument in data processing and a crucial stage in the scientific method. They serve as a basis for more complex statistical procedures and guarantee that data is well comprehended prior to inferential analysis. Descriptive statistics aid in the identification of patterns, trends, and anomalies by summarizing and visualizing data, which directs additional analysis and decision-making.

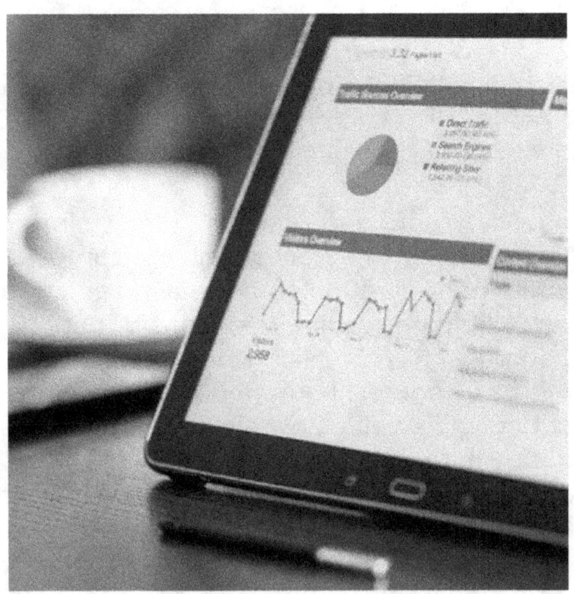

The importance of descriptive statistics in the context of big data and data science cannot be overstated. With the volume, diversity, and velocity of data continuing to expand, the capacity to quickly and effectively summarize and understand data becomes increasingly important. Data scientists and analysts can obtain insights and pinpoint areas for more research by using descriptive statistics to condense huge and complicated datasets into insightful summaries.

Descriptive statistics now have more power thanks to technological developments. Programming languages and software tools like R, Python, and SPSS provide robust functions and packages for doing descriptive statistical analysis. By enabling analysts to work with huge datasets, automate tedious processes, and produce intricate visualizations, these technologies improve the accessibility and efficiency of the descriptive statistics process.

Moreover, new directions in data analysis have been made possible by the fusion of machine learning, artificial intelligence (AI), and descriptive statistics. Before using machine learning techniques, descriptive statistics can be used to preprocess and examine the data to make sure it is clear and well-understood. Additionally, by spotting patterns and relationships that conventional methods might miss, machine learning techniques can improve descriptive statistics.

The idea of data normalization is a critical component of descriptive statistics. In order to facilitate comparison and analysis, data normalization entails scaling and translating data into a standard format. Log transformation, z-score normalization, and min-max scaling are examples of normalizing procedures. Min-max scaling involves taking the most negligible value and dividing it by the range to fit the data within a given range, usually 0 to 1. Z-score normalization is appropriate for algorithms that presume normally distributed data since it changes the data to have a mean of zero and a standard deviation of one. By using the logarithm function to the data, log transformation lessens the effect of extreme values and can assist in normalizing distributions and stabilizing variance.

Additionally essential to process optimization and quality control are descriptive statistics. Descriptive statistics are used in manufacturing and production to track and manage product quality, find flaws, and streamline procedures. Process performance can be improved by utilizing methods like control charts, Pareto analysis, and process capability analysis, which offer insightful information. For instance, control charts show data points plotted over time together with allowable variability indicated by control limits. Manufacturers can identify changes or patterns in the process and implement remedial measures to preserve quality by keeping an eye on control charts.

Descriptive statistics are used in education to evaluate educational results, examine student performance, and guide policy choices. Test results, graduation rates, and other measures of academic accomplishment are summarized by educators and researchers using metrics of central tendency and variability. Trends in student performance, such as the distribution of grades or the correlation between attendance and test results, can be seen through the use of graphic tools. Additionally, descriptive statistics support the assessment of educational interventions and programs' efficacy, directing initiatives to enhance instruction and student learning.

Descriptive statistics are crucial to the analysis of data on pollution, climate change, and natural resources in environmental research. These statistics are used by researchers to condense and analyze data from field investigations, satellite photography, and sensors. The central tendency and variability measures shed light on temperature patterns, biodiversity, and air quality. The use of graphic tools makes it easier to see how the environment has changed throughout time and in different places. The creation of models and simulations to forecast future environmental changes and guide policy decisions is further supported by descriptive statistics.

Descriptive statistics are used in finance to evaluate investment performance, manage risk, and examine market data. Financial analysts summarize stock prices, interest rates, and economic indicators using measures of central tendency and variability—graphical methods aid in the visualization of market patterns, including changes in price and volume of trades. Descriptive statistics are also useful for portfolio management since they assist investors assess the risk and return characteristics of different assets and make educated investment decisions.

In the discipline of sports analytics, descriptive statistics are also essential since they help assess player performance, examine game plans, and guide coaching choices. A player's scoring, batting, and shooting percentages, among other player statistics, can be understood using measures of central tendency and variability. Shot charts and heat maps are two examples of graphic tools that are used to visualize player and team performance. In order to guide decisions about team makeup and tactics, descriptive statistics are also used to support the development of predictive models that forecast player performance and game outcomes.

Descriptive statistics are crucial for epidemiology and public health as well since they are used to track disease outbreaks, rate health-related behaviors, and analyze treatments. To summarize statistics on illness incidence, prevalence, and mortality, public health experts employ metrics of central tendency and variability. Geographic maps and epidemic curves are two examples of graphic approaches that are used to show the spread of illnesses. The discovery of disease risk factors, the evaluation of public health initiatives, and the measurement of healthcare access and utilization are all aided by descriptive statistics.

Descriptive statistics are used in marketing and consumer research to examine trends, preferences, and behavior of consumers. Marketers describe survey results, sales numbers, and market groups using metrics of central tendency and variability. Charts showing customer satisfaction and preference maps are examples of graphic approaches that aid in visualizing consumer preferences. Additionally helpful in market segmentation, descriptive statistics enable marketers to pinpoint certain customer groups and adjust their marketing tactics accordingly.

Descriptive statistics are used in political science to examine the effects of policies, public opinion, and election outcomes. Measures of central tendency and variability are used by political analysts to compile information about legislative activity, voter behavior, and approval ratings. Election results, including vote distributions and electoral maps, can be seen through the use of graphic tools. In addition to helping to guide decisions on public policy and governance, descriptive statistics are also helpful in analyzing political trends and assessing the efficacy of policies.

To summarize, measures of central tendency, variability, shape, and graphical representations are used in descriptive statistics, which is a fundamental branch of statistical analysis, to summarize and characterize data. These methods offer insightful analyses of data, facilitating the discovery of patterns, trends, and anomalies in a variety of domains. Descriptive statistics are crucial for comprehending and interpreting data, directing more research, and assisting in decision-making, even though they do not permit generalizations beyond the dataset. Descriptive statistics are becoming more and more valuable in the big data and data science era as a result of technological advancements and their integration with AI and machine learning.

Inferential statistics

The foundation of statistical analysis is inferential statistics, which enables analysts and researchers to derive significant inferences and make defensible choices from data gathered from a sample. Inferential statistics build on these findings to draw conclusions about a broader population, in contrast to descriptive statistics, which condense and characterize data within a sample. The purpose of this section is to examine the methods, importance, and applications of inferential statistics in a variety of fields, delving into their subtleties.

The idea of probability is fundamental to inferential statistics since it provides the framework for drawing conclusions about populations from sample data. A framework for measuring uncertainty and determining the likelihood of various events is provided by probability theory. Probability distributions are essential for modeling and evaluating data in inferential statistics. The normal distribution, which depicts continuous data with a symmetric, bell-shaped curve, and the binomial distribution, which represents the likelihood of success or failure in a sequence of independent trials, are the two most widely used probability distributions.

Making judgments about population parameters based on sample data is known as hypothesis testing, and it is one of the core methods of inferential statistics. The process of testing a hypothesis involves formulating two hypotheses: an alternative hypothesis that proposes a particular difference or effect and a null hypothesis that asserts that there is no significant difference or impact. Then, information is collected from a sample, and statistical procedures are utilized to determine if the results that are observed may be solely attributed to chance. In the event that the data are statistically significant, indicating a low likelihood of occurring by chance, the null hypothesis is discarded in favor of the alternative hypothesis.

Confidence intervals, which offer a range of values within which the valid population parameter is expected to fall, are another essential idea in inferential statistics. Confidence intervals, which represent the uncertainty involved in estimating population parameters from a sample, are created using sample data. The sample size and the researcher's selected level of confidence determine the width of the confidence interval. A 95% confidence interval, for instance, shows that there is a 95% chance that the proper population parameter falls inside the range.

Modeling the link between one or more independent variables and a dependent variable is done with regression analysis, another effective technique in inferential statistics. Regression analysis allows researchers to test theories about the effects of different elements, forecast future events, and assess the direction and strength of correlations. The most popular type of regression analysis, linear regression, uses a straight line to model the relationship between variables. On the other hand, nonlinear regression makes use of curves or other nonlinear functions to model more intricate relationships.

Analysis of variance (ANOVA), which is used to compare means across several groups or treatments, is also included in the category of inferential statistics. ANOVA enables researchers to find disparities between groups and test hypotheses on mean equality. When there is only one independent variable with three or more levels, one-way ANOVA is utilized; when there are two or more independent variables, factorial ANOVA is employed. In experimental research, ANOVA is frequently used to evaluate the impact of several treatments or interventions on an outcome variable.

Applications of inferential statistics are found in a wide range of fields, including business, social sciences, healthcare, and scientific research. Inferential statistics are used in scientific research to assess experimental findings, test hypotheses, and derive conclusions about underlying processes. For instance, inferential statistics are used by medical and public health researchers to evaluate the effectiveness of novel medications, compare treatment outcomes, and pinpoint disease risk factors. By analyzing data on pollution, biodiversity loss, and climate change, inferential statistics are employed in environmental science to assist researchers in making sense of the effects of human activity on the environment and guide policy decisions.

Inferential statistics are essential for financial analysis, market research, and decision-making in business and economics. Inferential statistics are used by marketing analysts to assess the success of advertising campaigns, segment the market, and examine consumer behavior. Inferential statistics are used by financial analysts to evaluate investment prospects, predict market trends, and control risk. Inferential statistics are used in operations management to lower costs, enhance quality, and optimize processes. For instance, the Six Sigma approach improves product quality and customer happiness by identifying and eliminating manufacturing process flaws through the use of inferential statistics.

Inferential statistics are used in the social sciences to examine survey data, experiment outcomes, and observational research. Sociologists use inferential statistics to evaluate theories about social phenomena, such as the relationship between socioeconomic status and health outcomes or the impact of social policy on inequality. Inferential statistics is a tool used by psychologists to investigate the causes of human behavior, evaluate the efficacy of psychotherapy interventions, and pinpoint risk factors for mental disease. Inferential statistics is a tool used by political scientists to examine election outcomes, gauge popular sentiment, and measure the effects of policy changes.

Inferential statistics are used in education to evaluate educational programs, assess student performance, and guide policy decisions. When comparing test results across several groups, such as children with varying learning needs or socioeconomic backgrounds, educators utilize inferential statistics. Researchers assess the efficacy of curriculum changes, interventions, and instructional strategies using inferential statistics. Inferential statistics are used by policy makers in the allocation of resources, setting of performance goals, and tracking of educational objectives.

Inferential statistics are used in the healthcare industry to evaluate healthcare interventions, determine illness risk factors, and evaluate the efficacy of medical treatments. Clinicians use inferential statistics to evaluate the efficacy and safety of new drugs, analyze data from clinical trials, and make evidence-based treatment decisions.Inferential statistics is a tool that epidemiologists use to study disease outbreaks, locate infection sources, and evaluate the effectiveness of public health initiatives. Inferential statistics is a tool used by health economists to assess the cost-effectiveness of healthcare interventions, distribute resources, and guide policy decisions.

In conclusion, inferential statistics is essential to statistical analysis because it allows analysts and researchers to draw conclusions about populations from sample data. By using methods like regression analysis, analysis of variance, confidence intervals, and hypothesis testing, inferential statistics offers a framework for deriving significant findings, testing hypotheses, and arriving at well-informed decisions in a variety of fields. With its wide range of applications in business, social sciences, healthcare, and scientific research, it is an essential tool in the toolbox of data-driven decision-making. The significance of inferential statistics is anticipated to rise in tandem with the volume and complexity of data, spurring advancements in statistical methodology and analysis approaches.

Probability theory

The mathematical foundation for measuring uncertainty and examining random events is provided by probability theory. It offers a strict framework for comprehending and projecting the probability of different events, serving as the basis for statistical inference and making decisions in the face of uncertainty. The goal of this section is to examine probability theory's complexities by delving into its foundational ideas, research methods, and various applications.

The idea of probability, which measures the possibility that events will occur, is the foundation of probability theory. A number between 0 and 1, which denotes impossibility (the event will never happen) and certainty (the event will always happen), is the probability of an event. Degrees of uncertainty are represented by probabilities between 0 and 1, where a more significant probability denotes more likelihood. By giving researchers and analysts guidelines and principles for computing probabilities, probability theory enables them to make well-informed decisions about uncertain events.

The sample space, or set of all possible outcomes of a random experiment, is one of the basic ideas in probability theory. For instance, the numbers 1 through 6 make up the sample space when rolling a six-sided die. Events are portions of the sample space that correspond to particular results or combinations of results. The percentage of outcomes in the sample space that match the event is the probability of that event. For instance, since there is only one possible result that corresponds to rolling a 3 out of six, the chance of rolling a three on a six-sided die is 1/6.

The rules and concepts of probability theory can also be used to combine probabilities and determine the likelihood of compound events. According to the addition rule, the possibility of two events coming together is equal to the sum of their respective probabilities, less the likelihood that they will intersect. For example, with a six-sided die, the possibility of rolling a four or a six (1/6), less the odds of rolling a 2, 4, or 6 (1/6 plus 1/6 plus 1/6), is the possibility of rolling an even number or a number bigger than 4. According to the multiplication rule, the likelihood that two independent occurrences would meet equals the sum of their respective probabilities. For instance, the possibility of rolling a two on the first die (1/6) and a three on the second die (1/6), multiplied by each other, equals 1/36 for the probability of rolling a two on one die and a three on another.

Another key idea in probability theory is conditional probability, which measures the chance of an event given the occurrence of another event. The likelihood of the intersection of events A and B divided by the chance of event B is known as the conditional probability of event A given event B, or P(A|B). When rolling an odd number (1 or 3), for example, only one of the two possible results is equal to moving a 3. Consequently, assuming that the number rolled is odd, the conditional probability of rolling a three on a six-sided die is 1/3. To update beliefs and create predictions based on fresh data, conditional probability is an essential component of Bayesian inference.

The foundation of probability theory is probability distributions, which offer a quantitative explanation of the chance of various outcomes for a given random variable. A variable is said to be random if the result of a random experiment determines its value. Probability distributions can be either way, depending on whether the random variable takes on discrete or continuous values. Probabilities are assigned to individual outcomes by discrete probability distributions and to intervals of values by continuous probability distributions. For discrete distributions, the probabilities associated with various values of a random variable are described by mathematical functions called the probability mass function (PDF) and probability density function (PMF), respectively.

The most widely used probability distribution is the normal distribution, also known as the bell curve or the Gaussian distribution. It characterizes continuous data as having a symmetric, bell-shaped curve. The mean, which indicates the distribution's central tendency, and the standard deviation, which indicates the distribution's dispersion or variability, are the two characteristics that define a normal distribution. The normal distribution is a crucial idea in probability theory and statistics because many natural occurrences roughly follow them. The Poisson distribution, which indicates the chance of a particular number of events occurring in a predefined interval of time or space, and the binomial distribution, which expresses the chance of a certain amount of achievements in a fixed amount of autonomous trials, are two different necessary probability distributions. Numerous fields and businesses, including finance, economics, science, and engineering, use probability theory applications. Probability theory is used in science and engineering to describe and evaluate random occurrences, including weather patterns, particle motion, and radioactive decay. A mathematical foundation for comprehending and forecasting the behavior of complex systems is provided by probability distributions, which help to guide actions and decisions aimed at reducing risk and uncertainty. Probability theory is used in finance and economics to evaluate investment prospects, predict market trends, and control risk. Probability distributions are used by financial analysts to optimize portfolio allocation methods, simulate asset returns, and assess the likelihood of various investment outcomes. Probability theory is applied in medicine and healthcare to evaluate healthcare interventions, determine illness risk factors, and assess the effectiveness of medical treatments. Probability distributions are used by epidemiologists to predict illness prevalence, model the spread of infectious diseases, and guide public health initiatives.

In conclusion, probability theory provides the mathematical framework for assessing uncertainty and studying chance events. Its ideas and tenets offer a strict framework for comprehending and projecting the probability of different events, serving as the foundation for statistical inference and making decisions in the face of uncertainty. In numerous domains and disciplines, probability theory provides a comprehensive toolkit for modeling and understanding random processes, ranging from the sample space and events to probability distributions and conditional probability. Its uses drive innovation and improvement in our understanding of the world around us, spanning science, engineering, finance, healthcare, and other fields. Probability theory will only become more significant as data volume and complexity rise, solidifying its place as a critical instrument in the toolbox of scientific research and data-driven decision-making.

Hypothesis testing

A fundamental component of statistical analysis, hypothesis testing provides a methodical framework for judgments and inferences based on sample data. The rigorous methodology of hypothesis testing, which has its roots in probability theory, is utilized to evaluate the validity of conjectures and hypotheses regarding population parameters. The purpose of this section is to examine the complexities of hypothesis testing by delving into its foundational ideas, methods, and applications in various industries.

The creation and assessment of hypotheses regarding population parameters form the basis of hypothesis testing. A conjecture or assumption regarding the value of a population parameter, like the population mean or proportion, is called a hypothesis. Testing two opposing hypotheses, the alternative hypothesis (Ha) and the null hypothesis (H0), is known as hypothesis testing. The alternative hypothesis proposes a particular difference or effect, while the null hypothesis, which states that there is no substantial difference or impact, represents the status quo or default assumption.

Null and alternative hypotheses are first developed, and then sample data is gathered to start the hypothesis testing procedure. The evidence against the null hypothesis is then evaluated by researchers using statistical tests to see if it is more likely than not that the observed outcomes are the result of pure chance. A p-value, which measures the strength of the evidence against the null hypothesis, is the result of a hypothesis test. Strong evidence against the null hypothesis is shown by a small p-value, which leads to the alternative hypothesis' rejection.

The significance level, represented by α (alpha), is a basic idea in hypothesis testing. It is the highest likelihood of making a Type I error. When the null hypothesis is rejected even when it is true, a Type I error takes place, and a false positive conclusion is reached. The researcher determines the appropriate balance between Type I and Type II mistakes to determine the significance level α. $\alpha = 0.05$ and $\alpha = 0.01$ are often utilized significance thresholds, signifying a 5% and 1% likelihood of committing a Type I error, respectively.

The test statistic, a numerical summary of the sample data used to evaluate the evidence against the null hypothesis, is another essential idea in hypothesis testing. Since every test figure under the null condition follows a known probability distribution, researchers can calculate the likelihood of discovering a test statistic as extreme as the one produced from the sample data itself. Test statistics that are frequently employed include the chi-square statistic, which is used to test hypotheses about categorical data, and the z- and t-statistics, which are used to test hypotheses about population means.

Since the p-value indicates the strength of the evidence against the null hypothesis, its interpretation is crucial to the process of hypothesis testing. A low p-value, usually less than the selected significance level α, suggests substantial evidence refuting the null hypothesis and supporting the alternative hypothesis. A high p-value, on the other hand, denotes insufficient evidence to challenge the null hypothesis, maintaining it. The p-value indicates the probability of discovering the sample data or something more extreme, assuming the null hypothesis is true.

One of two conclusions may arise from a hypothesis test: either the null hypothesis is rejected, or it is not rejected. The alternative hypothesis is accepted and the null hypothesis is rejected if the p-value is less than the significance level α, suggesting that the observed data are statistically significant. The null hypothesis is kept if the p-value is higher than the significance level α since there is not enough data to reject it. It is important to realize that failing to reject the null hypothesis does not imply acceptance of the null hypothesis because there may not be sufficient data to reach a firm conclusion.

Applications for hypothesis testing can be found in many different domains and disciplines, including business, social sciences, healthcare, and scientific research. Testing hypotheses is a method used in scientific research to assess experimental findings, verify theoretical predictions, and derive inferences about underlying processes. To evaluate the effectiveness of novel medications, compare treatment outcomes, and pinpoint disease risk factors, for instance, researchers in the fields of medicine and public health employ hypothesis testing. In environmental science, data on pollution, biodiversity loss, and climate change are analyzed using hypothesis testing to assist researchers in understanding how human activity affects the environment and guide policy decisions.

Hypothesis testing is a tool used in business and economics to analyze marketing plans, identify market trends, and allocate resources wisely. Marketing analysts compare customer preferences, determine market segmentation, and evaluate the success of advertising efforts using hypothesis testing. To analyze investment opportunities, predict market trends, and gauge the effects of economic policies, financial analysts employ hypothesis testing. Hypothesis testing is used in operations management to streamline workflows, raise standards, and cut expenses. For instance, the Six Sigma technique makes use of hypothesis testing to find and fix flaws in production processes, which enhances the caliber of the final product and increases customer satisfaction.

Hypothesis testing is a technique used in the social sciences to examine survey data, experiment results, and observational studies. To evaluate theories concerning social phenomena, such as the connection between socioeconomic status and health outcomes or the influence of social policies on inequality, sociologists employ hypothesis testing. To determine risk factors for mental disease, evaluate the efficacy of therapeutic interventions, and investigate the elements that influence human behavior, psychologists employ hypothesis testing. Hypothesis testing is a tool used by political scientists to examine the effects of policy initiatives, gauge public sentiment, and analyze election results.

Hypothesis testing is a tool used in education to evaluate educational programs, assess student performance, and guide policy decisions. Hypothesis testing is a useful tool used by educators to evaluate test results between groups, such as pupils with varied learning requirements or socioeconomic backgrounds. Researchers assess the efficacy of curriculum changes, treatments, and instructional strategies using hypothesis testing. Hypothesis testing is a tool used by policymakers to determine performance goals, distribute funds, and track advancement toward educational objectives.

Hypothesis testing is used in the medical field to evaluate healthcare interventions, determine disease risk factors, and gauge the effectiveness of medical treatments. To assess the safety and efficacy of novel medications, examine clinical trial data, and make evidence-based treatment decisions, clinicians employ hypothesis testing. To investigate disease outbreaks, locate infection sources, and evaluate the effectiveness of public health initiatives, epidemiologists employ hypothesis testing. Hypothesis testing is a tool used by health economists to assess the cost-effectiveness of healthcare interventions, distribute resources, and guide the formulation of public policy.

To sum up, hypothesis testing offers a methodical framework for judgments and inferences based on sample data. A rigorous process for evaluating the evidence against conjectures and hypotheses concerning population parameters is provided by hypothesis testing, which includes the formulation of null and alternative hypotheses, the computation of test statistics, and the interpretation of p-values. With its wide range of applications in business, social sciences, healthcare, and scientific research, it is an essential tool for data-driven decision-making and statistical inference. As data volume and complexity increase, hypothesis testing is expected to become ever more important, strengthening its position in knowledge progress and decision-making across a broad spectrum of fields.

CHAPTER IV

Basic Concepts of Machine Learning

Supervised vs. unsupervised learning

Both supervised and unsupervised learning are the two primary methodologies and approaches in machine learning, each with specific uses. These methods are essential for gleaning information and patterns from data, which makes it possible to perform operations like dimensionality reduction, clustering, regression, and classification. The purpose of this section is to examine the nuances of both supervised and unsupervised learning, including its underlying theories, practical applications, and methods.

A model is trained with labeled data in supervised learning, where each sample is associated with a desired variable or outcome. By creating a mapping from input variables to output variables, supervised learning seeks to enable the algorithm to make recommendations on new, unknown information. Input-output pairs—where the input variables act as features or predictors and the output variable acts as the target variable to be predicted—make up the training data for supervised learning. Regression and classification are everyday tasks in supervised learning, where the objective is to predict a continuous outcome variable and assign inputs to predetermined classes or categories.

When given enough labeled data, supervised learning may learn intricate patterns and correlations between input and output variables, which is one of its main advantages. Supervised learning methods use optimization techniques to reduce a negative value, which determines the distinction between the anticipated and actual values of the target variable. Supervised learning algorithms learn to make accurate predictions on fresh, unseen data by iteratively changing the model parameters. Applications for supervised learning can be found in many fields, including financial forecasting, medical diagnosis, natural language processing, and picture recognition.

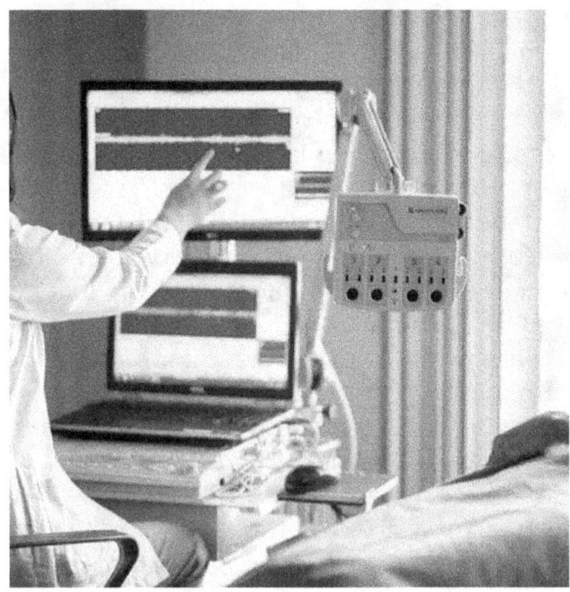

Unsupervised learning, on the other hand, entails training a model using unlabeled data, in which the goal variables or output labels do not correlate to the input variables. Unsupervised learning aims to find underlying structures, correlations, or patterns in the data without the need for direct supervision or direction. Because unsupervised learning approaches search for patterns, similarities, or contrasts in the data, they can be applied to tasks like grouping, anomaly detection, and dimensionality reduction.

The lack of ground truth labels in unsupervised learning is a significant obstacle that makes it challenging to assess the model's performance impartially.

Reconstruction error and clustering validity indices are two metrics that unsupervised learning systems use to evaluate the caliber of learned representations. Unsupervised learning, in spite of this difficulty, provides essential insights into the underlying structure of data by revealing correlations or patterns that may not be obvious from the raw input variables alone. Unsupervised learning is a crucial technique for data scientists, with applications in feature learning, data preparation, and exploratory data analysis.

Even though supervised and unsupervised learning is two different techniques of machine learning, they are frequently combined to solve challenging issues. They are using the availability of unlabeled data to augment the restricted amount of labeled data, and semi-supervised learning blends labeled and unlabeled data to improve model performance. A machine learning paradigm called reinforcement learning makes use of incentives or feedback from interactions with the environment to promote learning without the need for direct supervision. Reinforcement learning can be understood as either an unsupervised learning process in which the agent learns to explore and take advantage of its surroundings in order to maximize cumulative rewards or as a type of supervised learning in which the reward signal acts as the target variable.

To sum up, there are two main methods for machine learning: supervised and unsupervised learning. Each has advantages and disadvantages. Supervised learning uses labeled data to train a model to generate predictions on fresh, unseen data, whereas unsupervised learning searches unlabeled data for hidden patterns or structures. Both strategies are essential for deriving insights from data and facilitating processes like dimensionality reduction, clustering, regression, and classification. It is anticipated that the combination of supervised and unsupervised learning approaches will spur innovation and make it possible to create increasingly potent and adaptable machine learning systems as the field of machine learning develops.

Common algorithms and their applications

Algorithms are the cornerstone of modern computers and are required to solve a wide range of problems efficiently. Almost all aspects of digital technology rely on algorithms, from sorting and searching to machine learning and optimization. The purpose of this section is to examine a few popular algorithms and the wide range of uses they have in different fields.

The sorting algorithm, which puts a group of objects in a particular order, is among the most basic algorithms. Sorting algorithms come in a variety of forms, including bubble sort, insertion sort, selection sort, merge sort, and quicksort. The effectiveness, stability, and applicability of these methods to various data kinds vary. Extensive dataset sorting is a prevalent task in databases, operating systems, and information retrieval systems, all of which find use for sorting algorithms.

The search algorithm, which finds a particular item or value inside a collection of data, is another crucial algorithm. Hashing-based search algorithms, binary search, and linear search are examples of standard search algorithms. Linear search works well with unordered lists because it iteratively examines every element in the collection until the desired item is located. In contrast, binary search divides the search space in two regularly to find items in sorted lists quickly. Constant-time lookup operations are made possible by hash-based search algorithms, which map keys to array indices using hash functions. Search algorithms are used by databases, web search engines, and information retrieval systems to efficiently and rapidly locate relevant information.

Graph algorithms are a significant category of algorithms that are employed to represent the connections among elements inside a network. Graph algorithms comprise minimum spanning tree techniques like Prim's and Kruskal's, shortest path algorithms like Dijkstra's and Bellman-Ford's, and traversal algorithms like depth-first search (DFS) and breadth-first search (BFS). Graph algorithms are helpful in computer networking, social networks, and transportation networks where it's critical to analyze and optimize connectivity.

Algorithms such as machine learning allow computers to learn from data and come to conclusions or predictions without the need for explicit programming. Supervised learning approaches include logistic regression, neural networks, random forests, decision trees, support vector machines (SVM), and linear regression. In order to generate predictions or categorize fresh data points into predetermined groups, these algorithms learn from labeled data. Unsupervised learning approaches include k-means clustering, hierarchical clustering, autoencoders, and principal component analysis (PCA). These algorithms enable tasks like clustering, dimensionality reduction, and anomaly detection by identifying underlying patterns or structures in unlabeled data. Applications for machine learning algorithms can be found in many domains where predictive modeling and pattern identification are crucial, such as finance, healthcare, marketing, and robotics.

Algorithms that discover the best option within a range of workable solutions for a given problem are known as optimization algorithms. Particle swarm optimization, simulated annealing, gradient descent, and genetic algorithms are examples of standard optimization techniques. These methods optimize objective functions by iteratively searching the solution space and modifying model parameters to minimize or maximize the objective function. Several disciplines, including operations research, engineering design, and financial modeling, use optimization approaches to identify the best answer to challenging issues.

Algorithms that compress data by encoding it in a more adequate representation are known as compression algorithms. Huffman coding, run-length encoding, and Lempel-Ziv-Welch (LZW) compression are examples of standard compression algorithms. These methods accomplish compression ratios without sacrificing information by taking advantage of patterns and redundancies in the data. Applications for compression techniques can be found in data transfer, storage, and multimedia applications where it's crucial to reduce bandwidth or storage needs.

Data is secured via encryption methods, which encrypt it in a way that can only be unlocked with the correct key. RSA (Rivest-Shamir-Adleman) and ECC (Elliptic Curve Cryptography) are examples of asymmetric encryption algorithms. Symmetric encryption techniques include DES (Data Encryption Standard) and AES (Advanced Encryption Standard). These algorithms offer sensitive data in storage and communication secrecy, integrity, and authentication. Applications for encryption algorithms can be found in digital signatures, secure communication, and data protection, all of which depend on keeping confidential information safe from unwanted access or alteration.

In summary, algorithms are essential components of computing and are necessary for effectively resolving a variety of issues. Almost all aspects of digital technology rely on algorithms, from sorting and searching to machine learning and optimization. In the digital age, we can use ordinary algorithms to solve complicated issues, spur creativity, and expand knowledge by being aware of their wide range of applications.

Model training and evaluation

The foundation of machine learning is model training and evaluation, which offers an organized framework for creating and evaluating prediction models. In these procedures, a model is trained on labeled data to identify patterns and relationships, and then its performance is assessed on unseen data to determine how well it can generalize. The purpose of this section is to examine the underlying ideas, approaches, and best practices of model training and evaluation, delving into their complexities.

The first step in model training is choosing a suitable algorithm or model architecture depending on the particular problem and the properties of the data. When labeled data is available, supervised learning techniques, including neural networks, support vector machines (SVM), decision trees, and linear regression, are frequently utilized for predictive modeling applications. Principal component analysis (PCA), hierarchical clustering, k-means clustering, and other unsupervised learning techniques are used in a variety of activities, including clustering, dimensionality reduction, and anomaly detection. The next stage is to train the model using labeled data to discover patterns and correlations between input characteristics and target variables after an algorithm or model architecture has been selected.

In order to minimize a loss function, which calculates the difference between the target variable's actual and anticipated values, the training procedure entails adjusting the model's parameters. Stochastic gradient descent, Adam, and gradient descent are examples of optimization techniques that are commonly used iteratively to update model parameters. These techniques are based on the inclination of the impairment value concerning the parameters. Usually, mini-batches are created from the training data in order to expedite optimization and enhance convergence. The number of training iterations, or epochs, is another hyperparameter that impacts the model's performance and is usually selected using hyperparameter tweaking or cross-validation.

The next stage is to test the model's performance with untrained data to determine how well it generalizes. The evaluation of a model involves determining performance metrics for each task: R-squared for regression tasks, recall, F1 score, mean absolute error (MAE), root mean square error (RMSE), area under the receiver operating characteristic (ROC) curve (AUC-ROC) for classification tasks, and mean squared error (MSE) for mean absolute error (MAE). These metrics can be used to compare various models or hyperparameter setups and offer quantitative evaluations of the model's prediction performance.

A popular method for evaluating models is called cross-validation, in which the training data is split up into folds or subsets, and the model is trained and assessed independently on each fold. The actual performance of the model is then estimated using the average performance over all folds. By minimizing the possibility of overfitting—a situation in which the model learns to memorize the training data rather than generalize to new, unknown data—cross-validation aids in evaluating the resilience of the model. For the evaluation of models, other methods, including holdout validation, k-fold cross-validation, and leave-one-out cross-validation, are also frequently employed.

To comprehend the underlying patterns and correlations that the model learns, model interpretation and visualization approaches are just as crucial as performance measurements. To understand the contributions of different features to the model's predictions, feature importance scores, partial dependence plots, and SHAP (Shapley Additive exPlanations) values are frequently utilized methodologies. The correlations between input features and target variables are visualized, and patterns or anomalies in the data are found using visualization techniques, including scatter plots, histograms, and heatmaps.

Marketing, finance, healthcare, and cybersecurity are just a few of the industries that use models for training and evaluation. Predictive models are utilized in healthcare for activities including patient risk classification, disease diagnosis, and treatment result prediction. Predictive models are used in finance to perform tasks like fraud detection, credit rating, and stock price forecasting. Predictive models are used in marketing for activities, including recommendation systems, churn prediction, and consumer segmentation. Predictive models are utilized in cybersecurity for activities like malware, phishing, and intrusion detection.

To sum up, machine learning requires both model training and model evaluation in order to provide a methodical framework for creating and evaluating predictive models. These procedures, which range from choosing a suitable algorithm or model architecture to optimizing model parameters and assessing model performance, combine computational tools, statistical methods, and domain expertise. Data scientists and machine learning practitioners may create reliable prediction models that work well across a variety of domains and applications by grasping the core ideas and best practices of model training and evaluation.These models will also generalize well to new, unknown data.

CHAPTER V

Tools and Technologies

Programming languages (Python, R)

Two of the most well-known programming languages in the fields of statistics, machine learning, and data science are Python and R. For data analysis, visualization, and modeling; both languages provide robust libraries, ecosystems, and tools. This section aims to investigate the unique features, benefits, and applications of the Python and R programming languages, along with their impact on data-driven decision-making and scientific research.

Python's readability, flexibility, and ease of use make it a popular language for data research and machine learning. Python offers a robust set of tools for data manipulation, analysis, and visualization thanks to its extensive ecosystem of libraries, which includes NumPy, pandas, matplotlib, and sci-kit-learn. NumPy is perfect for numerical computing and scientific computing jobs since it supports mathematical functions and multidimensional arrays. Data cleaning, transformation, and aggregation are made possible by pandas' high-performance data structures and analysis tools. For the purpose of producing static, interactive, and publication-quality visuals, Matplotlib provides an extensive set of charting tools. Numerous machine learning tools and methods, including those for clustering, regression, classification, and dimensionality reduction, are available with sci-kit-learn.

Python is versatile and may be used not only for data research but also for web development, software development, scripting, and automation. Python allows web apps, APIs, and microservices to be developed quickly thanks to frameworks like Django, Flask, and FastAPI. Building scalable and stable software solutions is made easier with Python's extensive standard library, simple syntax, and vibrant community support. Due in part to its popularity and ease of learning, Python is one of the most extensively used programming languages for data science and other sectors. It is also widely utilized in industry, academia, and open-source groups.

However, R is a domain-specific language created especially for data analysis and statistical computing. R has an extensive ecosystem of packages, including ggplot2, tidyverse, dplyr, and Caret, that offer solid capabilities for modeling, data manipulation, and visualization. tidyverse encourages a tidy data workflow and makes reproducible research more accessible by providing a set of uniform and unified tools for data manipulation, exploration, and visualization. A sophisticated and adaptable graphics grammar is offered by ggplot2 to enable the creation of excellent, fully customizable visualizations. The data manipulation tools provided by dplyr are quick and effective for tasks like filtering, summarizing, and merging datasets. Model selection, hyperparameter tuning, and performance evaluation are just a few of the functions that can be accomplished with Caret's unified interface for training and assessing machine learning models.

R is a good choice for tasks like exploratory data analysis, hypothesis testing, and statistical modeling because of its emphasis on statistical computing and data analysis. Researchers, statisticians, and data scientists in academia, government, and business choose it because of its broad support for statistical methods, algorithms, and procedures. R is widely used in scientific research and data-driven decision-making due to its emphasis on reproducibility, transparency, and cooperation. Its compatibility with R Markdown, knitr, and Shiny allows data analysis, reporting, and visualization to be seamlessly integrated, which facilitates communication and the sharing of research findings.

Despite having different uses and strengths, Python and R are frequently combined in complimentary ways to take advantage of the finest aspects of both languages. Python is a popular choice for activities like automation, web scraping, and data preprocessing because of its ease of integration and versatility. R is the tool of choice for activities like statistical modeling, hypothesis testing, and exploratory data analysis because of its emphasis on statistical computing and visualization. Interoperability between Python and R is made possible by tools like rpy2 and reticulate, which let users efficiently use the advantages of both languages in their data science operations.

To sum up, R and Python programming languages provide vital ecosystems, libraries, and tools designed for data science, statistics, and machine learning applications. For activities like data manipulation, analysis, and visualization, Python is a preferred option due to its ease of use, adaptability, and extensive ecosystem. R is a good choice for tasks like exploratory data analysis, hypothesis testing, and statistical modeling because of its emphasis on statistical computing and data analysis. Despite having different uses and strengths, Python and R are frequently combined in complimentary ways to take advantage of the finest aspects of both languages. Through an awareness of the distinct characteristics, benefits, and uses of the Python and R programming languages, analysts and data scientists may select the best tool for the task at hand and realize the full potential of their data-driven projects.

Libraries and frameworks (TensorFlow, Scikit-learn, PyTorch)

Libraries and frameworks that offer the necessary tools, algorithms, and capabilities to expedite the creation and implementation of predictive models are crucial to the progress of machine learning. Of the many options available, the machine learning community uses three popular libraries and frameworks that stand out: PyTorch, Scikit-learn, and TensorFlow. In order to shed light on TensorFlow, Scikit-learn, and PyTorch's contributions to the fields of artificial intelligence and data-driven decision-making, this section will examine the features, advantages, and applications of each framework.

The open-source machine learning framework TensorFlow, created by Google Brain, is renowned for its resilience, scalability, and adaptability. TensorFlow, which was developed with automatic differentiation and computational graphs, provides a flexible framework for creating and refining deep learning models. Its high-level APIs, like Keras, offer a user-friendly interface for creating and refining neural networks, facilitating quick experimentation and prototyping. Because of TensorFlow's distributed training features, users may scale their models across several GPUs or TPUs, which makes it appropriate for demanding machine learning applications like reinforcement learning, image recognition, and natural language processing. TensorFlow's extensive library and toolkit, which includes TensorFlow.js, TensorFlow Probability (TFP), and TensorFlow Extended (TFX), further expands its applicability to domains including web deployment, probabilistic modeling, and productionization.

A community of contributors created the Python library Scikit-learn, which is renowned for its elegance, use, and simplicity. For data preprocessing, feature engineering, model selection, and evaluation, Scikit-learn offers an extensive toolkit with an emphasis on conventional machine learning algorithms and methodologies. Its well-documented interface and consistent API make it usable by users of all skill levels. Many algorithms from Scikit-learn, including support vector machines, clustering algorithms, linear models, and tree-based models, can be used for a variety of applications, including dimensionality reduction, classification, regression, and clustering. Because of its focus on interpretability and simplicity, Scikit-learn is a popular choice among practitioners, educators, and academics who want to quickly prototype and implement machine learning solutions in a variety of sectors and domains.

The open-source machine learning framework PyTorch, created by Facebook AI Research, is renowned for its adaptable and dynamic computational graph. PyTorch is a Pythonic interface for neural network construction and training that was designed with deep learning in mind. It allows for eager execution, automatic differentiation, and dynamic computation graphs. Compared to static computational graphs, its dynamic nature offers greater expressiveness and flexibility, which makes it ideal for study, experimentation, and the quick development of novel algorithms. PyTorch is a top option for profound learning practitioners working on cutting-edge research and applications because of its smooth integration with Python libraries like NumPy and SciPy, support for GPU acceleration, and distributed training. Further expanding PyTorch's capabilities into computer vision, natural language processing, and transfer learning is its expanding ecosystem of libraries and tools, which includes torchvision, torchtext, and transformers.

Despite having different capabilities and advantages, Scikit-learn, PyTorch, and TensorFlow are frequently combined in complementary ways to take advantage of the best of both worlds. TensorFlow is a good choice for large-scale machine learning workloads and deployment in production contexts because of its scalability and production readiness. Scikit-learn is a recommended option for classical machine learning algorithm prototyping and experimentation due to its ease of use and simplicity. PyTorch is perfect for deep learning and artificial intelligence research, experimentation, and innovation because of its dynamic and flexible nature.

In summary, there are three well-known libraries and frameworks in the machine learning ecosystem: TensorFlow, Scikit-learn, and PyTorch. Each has its own advantages, capabilities, and uses. TensorFlow is appropriate for large-scale machine learning workloads and deployment in production environments due to its scalability, flexibility, and production readiness. Scikit-learn is a recommended option for traditional machine learning algorithm design and experimentation due to its elegance, simplicity, and ease of use. PyTorch is perfect for deep learning and artificial intelligence research, experimentation, and innovation because of its dynamic nature, adaptability, and Pythonic interface. Through a grasp of the characteristics, advantages, and uses of Scikit-learn, PyTorch, and TensorFlow, machine learning professionals may select the best tool for the task at hand and realize the full potential of their data-driven projects.

Software and platforms (Jupyter Notebook, Google Colab)

Practical tools and platforms are essential for promoting cooperation, experimentation, and productivity in the fields of data science and machine learning. Jupyter Notebook and Google Colab stand out among the many options available as two well-known programs and platforms that data scientists and researchers use all around the world. In order to highlight Jupyter Notebook and Google Colab's benefits and features, as well as their contributions to data-driven decision-making and scientific research, this section will examine these tools' features.

The open-source web application Jupyter Notebook completely transforms how data scientists and academics work with code and data. Jupyter Notebook is an interactive computing environment that integrates code execution, text, equations, visualizations, and narrative documentation in a single document. It is based on the ideals of interactivity, reproducibility, and collaboration. Its ability to work with several computer languages, such as Python, R, Julia, and Scala, makes it a flexible tool for modeling, data analysis, and visualization. Jupyter Notebook's versatility is further enhanced by its integration with well-known libraries and frameworks like NumPy, pandas, matplotlib, sci-kit-learn, and TensorFlow.

Support for literate programming, which enables users to blend executable code with rich text, equations, and multimedia, is one of Jupyter Notebook's primary features. This method improves the clarity and transparency of analysis operations and encourages reproducible research. Users can construct dynamic and captivating dashboards and visualizations with Jupyter Notebook's interactive widgets and extensions, which facilitate customization and interactivity. Its interaction with collaboration platforms like GitHub and GitLab and version control systems like Git makes versioning and collaboration easier. This makes sharing, reviewing, and publishing notebooks a breeze.

Google Colab is a cloud-based Jupyter Notebook environment that provides free access to computing resources and preconfigured libraries to enhance productivity and collaboration. Google Colab, hosted on the Google Cloud Platform, offers a scalable and adaptable cloud environment for code execution, model training, and data analysis. Users may easily store, share, and work together on notebooks because of its interface with Google Drive, which facilitates versioning and real-time collaboration. Google Colab is appropriate for deep learning and large-scale machine learning projects since it supports GPU and TPU acceleration, which speeds up computation and training operations.

One of Google Colab's key benefits is that it can be easily integrated with additional Google tools, such as Google Drive, Google Calendar, Google Spreadsheets, and Google Cloud Storage, which are all used for data consumption, preservation, and querying. Large datasets stored in the Google Cloud Platform can be analyzed by users thanks to its interaction with Google BigQuery, which enables high-performance searching and analysis. Rich and expressive documentation is made possible by Google Colab's support for Markdown, LaTeX, and interactive widgets, which improves the readability and clarity of analysis procedures. Because of its seamless integration of machine learning pipelines and workflows with Google Cloud Platform services like BigQuery, TensorFlow, and AI Platform, users are empowered to create, train, and implement machine learning models at scale.

Despite having different capabilities and benefits, Jupyter Notebook and Google Colab are frequently combined in complementary ways to take advantage of the best of both worlds. For the purpose of testing, experimenting, and exploring data science workflows, Jupyter Notebook is the recommended option due to its versatility, extensibility, and support for numerous programming languages. Google Colab is the go-to option for large-scale machine learning model training, computing, and collaboration because of its scalability, seamless integration with Google Cloud Platform services, and free computational resource access. Through a comprehensive comprehension of the attributes, capabilities, and benefits of Jupyter Notebook and Google Colab, researchers and data scientists may select the most appropriate tool for their needs and realize the complete potential of their data-driven projects.

CHAPTER VI

Linear Regression

Simple linear regression

One of the core methods in the fields of statistics and machine learning is simple linear regression, which is an effective tool for modeling and forecasting the connection between two continuous variables. The purpose of this section is to examine the complexities of simple linear regression by delving into its foundational ideas, methods, presumptions, and applications.

In essence, basic linear regression uses a linear equation of the type y=mx+b, where y-intercept is represented by b and slope of the line by m, to depict the relationship between a dependent variable (often designated as y) and an independent variable (typically designated as x). In basic linear regression, the sum of squared differences between the expected and actual values of the dependent variable is minimized in order to find values of m and b that most closely match the observed data points.

There are several essential processes involved in the process of basic linear regression. First, scatter plots and correlation analysis are used to assess the relationship between the independent and dependent variables in order to determine whether a linear relationship exists. The next step, if a linear relationship is seen, is to use least squares regression, a popular technique for fitting a line to a collection of data points, to estimate the linear equation's parameters. Reducing the sum of squared discrepancies between the observed values of the dependent variable and the values predicted by the linear equation is the aim of least squares regression.

In basic linear regression, assumptions are fundamental since breaking them might result in estimates that are biased and forecasts that could be more trustworthy. Linearity, independence, homoscedasticity (constant variance of residuals), and normality of residuals are the primary presumptions of simple linear regression. According to the linearity assumption, the dependent and independent variables have a linear relationship, which means that changes in the dependent variable are proportionate to changes in the independent variable. The assumption of independence states that the residuals, or the variations between the values that were seen and those that were anticipated, are unrelated to one another. The assumption of homoscedasticity states that the residuals' variance is constant at all levels of the independent variable. The assumption of residual normality is a regularly distributed set of residuals.

Applications for simple linear regression can be found in many different sectors and domains, such as social sciences, healthcare, economics, and finance. Simple linear regression is a tool used in finance and economics to model the link between variables like interest rates and investment returns, stock prices and market indices, and price and demand. Simple linear regression is a tool used in the social sciences to examine the association between variables like age and voting behavior or education and income. Simple linear regression is used in the medical field to forecast health outcomes based on dietary, exercise, and drug regimens.

To sum up, basic linear regression is a fundamental method in machine learning and statistics that offers a straightforward yet effective means of describing and forecasting the relationship between two continuous variables. Data scientists and researchers can use basic linear regression to produce predictions, obtain insights, and guide decision-making in a variety of sectors and domains by being aware of its fundamentals, assumptions, methodology, and applications.

Multiple linear regression

A link between a dependent variable and two or more independent variables can be modeled and predicted using multiple linear regression, which is an extension of simple linear regression. The objective of this section is to examine the complexities of multiple linear regression, including its foundational ideas, methods, presumptions, and applications in a range of fields.

At its core, multiple linear regression seeks to model the relationship between a dependent variable y y and numerous independent variables x 1, x 2, . . . , xn X 1,X 2,...,X n using a linear equation of the form $y = b$ 0 combined with b 1 x 1 together with b 2 x 2 + a result . . + $bnxn$ y=b 0+the variable b 1x 1+the variable b 2x 2+...+the variable b nx n, where b 0 b 0 represents the y-intercept and b 1, b 2, . . . , bn b 1,b 2,...,b n represent the slopes of the respective independent variables. The goal of multiple linear regression is to minimize the sum of squared differences between the dependent variable's actual and predicted values by estimating the probabilities of the parameters that b0, b1, which stands for the variable b2,..., bb n.

Like simple linear regression, multiple linear regression methodology requires a few essential steps. The relationship between each independent variable and the dependent variable is first assessed using scatter plots, correlation analysis, and multicollinearity diagnostics in order to determine whether there is a linear relationship between the independent variables and whether there are any multicollinearity issues. The next step is to estimate the linear equation's parameters using least squares regression, a popular technique for fitting a plane or hyperplane to a multidimensional set of data points if a linear relationship is seen and multicollinearity is absent. The goal of least squares regression is to reduce the sum of squared differences between the dependent variable's observed values and those predicted by the linear equation.

In multiple linear regression, assumptions are essential since breaking them might result in skewed estimates and inaccurate forecasts. Linearity, independence, homoscedasticity (constant variance of residuals), normality of residuals, and lack of multicollinearity are the primary presumptions of multiple linear regression. Every independent and dependent variable has a linear connection, according to the linearity assumption. According to the assumption of independence, there is no correlation between the residuals. The assumption of homoscedasticity states that the residuals' variance is constant at all levels of the independent variables. The assumption of residual normality is a regularly distributed set of residuals. Inflated standard errors and unstable coefficient estimates may result from the assumption that there are no significant correlations between the independent variables, which is known as no multicollinearity.

Applications for multiple linear regression can be found in a wide range of disciplines, including the social sciences, healthcare, economics, and finance. Multiple linear regression is a tool used in economics and finance to model the link between variables, taking into consideration several factors that may influence the dependent variable. Examples of these relationships include income and education, GDP and unemployment rate, or stock prices and market indices. Numerous linear regression is a technique used in the social sciences to examine the complicated interactions between multiple predictors and determine the association between variables like voting behavior and demographics or environmental factors and health outcomes. Multiple linear regression is used in the medical field to forecast health outcomes while accounting for the complex interplay between genetic predisposition, medicine, exercise, food, and other factors.

As a result, multiple linear regression is a flexible and effective method for analyzing and forecasting the relationship between a number of independent factors and a dependent variable. Data scientists and researchers can use multiple linear regression to create predictions, obtain insights, and guide decision-making in a variety of sectors and domains by being aware of its fundamentals, assumptions, methodology, and applications.

Assumptions and diagnostics

Researchers and data scientists can model the relationship between variables and provide predictions by using regression analysis, which is a fundamental tool in the toolset of statistical and machine learning techniques.

Regression analysis's validity is dependent on a number of critical assumptions, and if any of them are violated, the results' dependability and interpretability may be jeopardized. The purpose of this section is to examine the nuances of assumptions and diagnostics in regression analysis, as well as their significance, consequences, and techniques for identification and correction.

The foundation of regression analysis is a set of presumptions that uphold the validity of the model. These presumptions include the following: multicollinearity is not present, residuals are average, linearity, independence, and homoscedasticity. According to the linearity assumption, the dependent and independent variables have a linear relationship, which means that changes in the dependent variable are proportionate to changes in the independent variable. The assumption of independence states that there should be no systematic pattern or correlation in the residuals, which are the disparities between the observed and predicted values. The residuals' distribution is constant throughout the range of the predictor variables because, in accordance with the homoscedasticity assumption, the residuals' variance is constant at all levels of the independent variables. Assuming that the residuals follow a symmetric bell-shaped distribution around zero or that they are normally distributed is known as the normality of the residuals assumption. The lack of multicollinearity suggests that there are no substantial correlations between the independent variables since excessive multicollinearity can lead to inflated standard errors and unstable coefficient estimations.

Finding breaches in these presumptions is essential to guaranteeing the reliability and validity of regression analysis findings. To evaluate the presumptions and identify any problems, a number of diagnostic methods and instruments are available. For instance, residual analysis looks for patterns or trends in the residuals or the disparities between the actual and anticipated values, which could point to assumptions being broken. Residual plots can highlight trends like nonlinearity, heteroscedasticity, or outliers. Examples of these plots are scatter plots of residuals against anticipated values or residuals against independent variables. Using standard probability plots, sometimes referred to as Q-Q plots, one can visually evaluate the residuals' normality by contrasting the observed residuals with those predicted by a normal distribution. In order to find significant data points that could significantly affect the regression findings, Cook's distance and leverage statistics are employed. These statistics may point to outliers or leverage points that require additional research. Higher VIF values indicate stronger correlations and possible multicollinearity issues. The examination of multicollinearity among the independent variables is done using correlation matrices and variance inflation factors (VIFs).

Depending on the type and seriousness of the problems found, there are a number of approaches that can be used to remedy assumption violations. Stabilizing variance and enhancing the linearity of the relationship can be achieved by transforming variables, for as, by taking the square root or logarithm of skewed variables. Heteroscedasticity can be taken into consideration in weighted least squares regression by giving data with more minor variances larger weights. Vital regression techniques, such as Huber or Tukey square regression, can be applied to eliminate or down weight outliers that might be influencing the outcomes. Regularization techniques such as LASSO regression and ridge regression penalize high coefficients and encourage sparsity in the model, which can be used to reduce multicollinearity. Regression alternatives like nonparametric or extended linear models may be taken into consideration if the assumptions need to be sufficiently addressed.

In summary, regression analysis offers a framework for assessing the validity and dependability of the results, but it also significantly depends on assumptions and diagnostics. Researchers and data scientists can ensure the integrity of their analyses and make well-informed decisions about the suitability of the regression model and the interpretation of its results by being aware of the underlying assumptions of regression analysis and using diagnostic tools and techniques to assess potential violations. Through appropriate transformations, weighting schemes, robust methods, regularization techniques, or alternative regression approaches, researchers can address assumption violations and improve the generalizability and robustness of their regression analyses, as well as extract valuable insights from their data.

CHAPTER VII

Classification Algorithms

Logistic regression

One crucial statistical technique for modeling binary outcome variables is logistic regression. Based on one or more independent factors, this method forecasts the likelihood of a dependent variable, which has two alternative outcomes. Unlike linear regression, which forecasts a continuous result, logistic regression is intended for scenarios in which the response variable is binary. Since its introduction in David Cox's work in 1958, logistic regression has been extensively used in a range of fields, including finance, the social sciences, medicine, and machine learning, due to its interpretability and ease of use.

The foundation of logistic regression is the logistic function, often known as the sigmoid function, which transforms any real number into a value between 0 and 1. This transformation is critical for modeling probability. The logistic function is defined as $\sigma(z) = \frac{1}{1 + e^{-z}}$, where z is a linear combination of the predictor variables. The logistic regression model $P(Y = 1 \mid \mathbf{x}) = \sigma(\mathbf{x}^T \mathbf{\beta}) = \frac{1}{1 + e^{-(\beta_0 + \beta_1 x_1 + \beta_2 x_2 + \cdots + \beta_p x_p)}}$ represents the likelihood that a given input $\mathbf{x}$ is a member of a specific class in logistic regression. The binary response variable, in this case, is denoted by Y, the predictor variable vector is represented by $\mathbf{x}$, and the coefficient vector is denoted by $\mathbf{\beta}$.

Maximal likelihood estimation (MLE) is commonly employed in logistic regression to estimate the coefficients $\mathbf{\beta}$. An independent set of n observations has the likelihood function $L(\mathbf{\beta}) = \prod_{i=1}^{n} P(y_i | \mathbf{x}_i; \mathbf{\beta})$. $\log L(\mathbf{\beta}) = \sum_{i=1}^{n} \left[y_i \log \sigma(\mathbf{x}_i^T \mathbf{\beta}) + (1 - y_i) \log (1 - \sigma(\mathbf{x}_i^T \mathbf{\beta})) \right]$. This log-likelihood is more convenient to compute. The model parameter estimations are obtained by maximizing the log-likelihood function with regard to $\mathbf{\beta}$.

Several requirements must be satisfied for logistic regression to produce accurate and trustworthy findings. First, the predictor variables and the outcome logit must have a linear relationship. For the likelihood estimation method to be valid, the observations must be independent of one another. Predictor variable multicollinearity should also be kept to a minimum since too much multicollinearity can provide estimates that are unstable. Reliable estimates also depend on a suitably high sample size and a binary dependent variable that can only take on values of 0 or 1.

Applications of logistic regression are widespread in many different fields. It is used to model the likelihood of an illness or condition based on risk variables in medical research. For instance, it can forecast a patient's risk of having a heart attack depending on factors including age, cholesterol, and smoking status. Logistic regression is a tool used in finance to evaluate a borrower's creditworthiness by forecasting the likelihood of a loan default based on their financial and personal attributes. It is used by marketing experts to predict consumer behavior, including the chance of a purchase or a campaign response. For machine learning applications like fraud detection, sentiment analysis, and spam detection, logistic regression is also widely used.

Logistic regression has significant drawbacks despite its benefits. Its presumption of linearity between the predictors and the outcome's log odds is one of its main limitations. Should this supposition be broken, the model's functionality may be compromised. Although expansions are available for multinomial and ordinal outcomes, the primary purpose of logistic regression is also for binary outcomes. Furthermore, imbalanced datasets, in which one class is significantly more frequent than the other, might cause logistic regression to perform poorly and produce biased results. Non-linear correlations between predictors and the outcome are another issue it struggles with, but this can be somewhat resolved by including polynomial and interaction variables.

In order to avoid overfitting in logistic regression, regularization techniques like L1 (Lasso) and L2 (Ridge) regularization are frequently utilized, particularly in models with a large number of predictors. These strategies strengthen the robustness of the model and decrease the size of the coefficients by appending a penalty to the log-likelihood function.

Finally, logistic regression, which provides straightforward, comprehensible, and probabilistic results, is an essential statistical technique for binary classification issues. It has many different applications in many different sectors. Although logistic regression has certain drawbacks, regularization and other methods can help to lessen these effects, giving it a flexible and practical approach for binary classification applications.

Support vector machines (SVM)

A potent collection of supervised learning techniques for regression, outlier identification, and classification is called Support Vector Machines (SVM). Especially for binary classification tasks, Support Vector Machines (SVM), first presented by Vladimir Vapnik and Alexey Chervonenkis in 1963, have grown to be one of the most widely used and reliable methods in machine learning. SVM's primary goal is to identify the hyperplane that maximizes the margin between classes while effectively dividing the data into distinct classes. SVM is very good at managing high-dimensional data and attaining high accuracy because of this margin maximization.

The idea of the hyperplane, a decision boundary that divides the data points into several classes, is the foundation of support vector machines (SVM). When addressing a binary classification problem, the goal is to find the hyperplane that minimizes the border, which refers to the span between the center a hyperplane and the closest data point from each class or support vector. The model's capacity for generalization improves with increasing margin. The weight vector is $\mathbf{w}$, the feature vector is $\mathbf{x}$, and the bias term is b. This is the mathematical definition of the hyperplane: $\mathbf{w} \cdot \mathbf{x} + b = 0$.

Convex optimization problems are solved by SVM in order to determine the ideal hyperplane. With the restriction that every data point be correctly classified with a margin of at least 1, the goal is to minimize the norm of the weight vector $||\mathbf{w}||$. This is a quadratic programming problem, to put it simply: reduce $\frac{1}{2} ||\mathbf{w}||^2$ in accordance with $y_i (\mathbf{w} \cdot \mathbf{x}_i + b) \geq one$, where y_i's class label corresponds to the i-th data point. When this problem is solved, the ideal hyperplane's parameters are obtained.

Using kernel functions, SVM can handle non-linearly separable data, which is one of its main characteristics. The original feature space is converted into a higher-dimensional space that allows for a linear separation using a kernel function. The linear, polynomial, sigmoid, and radial basis function (RBF) kernels are examples of frequently used kernel functions. The type of data and the particular issue at hand determine the kernel to use. The computation is more efficient because of the kernel approach, which enables SVM to carry out intricate transformations without explicitly calculating the coordinates in the high-dimensional space.

Additionally, SVM includes a regularization parameter, often represented as C, which manages the trade-off between minimizing the classification error and maximizing the margin. While a lower C value permits a broader margin and some misclassifications, a large C value places greater focus on accurately classifying all training instances, possibly at the expense of a smaller margin. Overfitting is avoided in part by this regularization, mainly when working with noisy data.

SVM has a plethora of benefits. Its efficacy in high-dimensional spaces is one of its main advantages, which makes it appropriate for applications with lots of characteristics. Because SVM defines the decision boundary using a subset of the training points (support vectors), it is also memory efficient. The method can be implemented with different kernel functions, which makes it flexible enough to handle both linear and non-linear classification issues. SVMs have been effectively used in a variety of domains, such as bioinformatics, handwriting recognition, and picture and text classification.

SVMs do have certain limits, though. The computational complexity of training the model is a significant downside, especially when dealing with massive datasets. It can take a lot of time and computing power to solve the quadratic optimization issue that is part of the training process. Furthermore, the selection of the kernel and its parameters have a significant impact on SVM performance. It frequently takes a lot of trial and error and cross-validation to choose the correct kernel and adjust its parameters as well as the regularization parameter (C). Additionally, when there are more features than samples, SVMs typically perform poorly—a situation referred to as the "curse of dimensionality."

SVM is still a potent and adaptable tool in the machine learning toolbox in spite of these drawbacks. It is a solid option for many applications due to its theoretical underpinnings in margin maximization and its capacity to tackle non-linear classification issues using kernel functions. The efficiency and scalability of SVM are continually being improved by advancements in computational resources and optimization techniques, which guarantees its continued relevance in the rapidly developing field of machine learning.

In conclusion, support vector machines are a powerful supervised learning technique that delivers strong classification performance and can handle large amounts of data. Using kernel functions for non-linear problems and optimizing the margin between classes, support vector machines (SVM) provide a flexible and effective method for a range of machine learning applications. The accuracy and generalization advantages of Support Vector Machines (SVM) render it a viable technique for both researchers and practitioners despite the demands of computing challenges and parameter tuning.

k-Nearest Neighbors (k-NN)

For classification and regression applications, the k-Nearest Neighbors (k-NN) algorithm is a straightforward, effective, and adaptable machine learning technique. This kind of instance-based learning postpones all computation until after the function has been evaluated. The function is approximated locally. The k-NN algorithm's origins are in early pattern recognition research, and because of its efficiency and simplicity, it has grown to be a vital tool in a number of fields, including computer vision, bioinformatics, and recommendation systems.

The main principle of k-NN is to classify a data point according to the classification of its neighbors. The k-training examples that are closest to a particular test instance in the feature space are found using k-NN in its most basic version. A majority vote among these k neighbors is then used to decide the classification. The forecast for regression tasks is usually computed as the mean of the values of the k nearest neighbors. Choosing k, taking into account the number of neighbors, and determining the distance between instances are the three main components of the k-NN algorithm.

The most common distance metric is the distance defined by Euclid, which is the square root of the total squared differences between comparable qualities of two instances. The Euclidean distance for two points in an n-dimensional space, denoted mathematically as x_i x i and x_i x j, is given by:

$$d(x_i, x_j) = \sum k = 1\, n\, (x_{ik} - x_g)$$

Two times $(x_i, x_j) = \sum k = 1\, n\, (x_{ik}, -x_{jk})$

Various other metrics for measuring distance, like the Manhattan, Minkowski, and Hamming distances, can also be employed based on the type of data and the particular issue at hand. Particularly in high-dimensional environments, the k-NN algorithm's performance can be significantly impacted by the distance metric selection.

Another crucial element in the effectiveness of k-NN is choosing a suitable value for k. Overfitting occurs when k is too small because the algorithm becomes more susceptible to noise in the training set. On the other hand, an excessively high value of k may cause the decision boundary to be overly smooth, which could result in underfitting. Using cross-validation, which involves evaluating the model's performance for several values of k on a validation set and selecting the value that produces the highest performance, is a popular method for determining the ideal k.

The simplicity and convenience of implementation of k-NN is one of its key benefits. Being non-parametric, it doesn't necessitate any presumptions regarding the distribution of the underlying data. This property enables k-NN to function well in a broad range of applications and adapt to different data distributions. Because the decision-making process is clear-cut and transparent and depends only on the labeled occurrences in the dataset, k-NN is also naturally interpretable.

Nevertheless, there are a few significant disadvantages to k-NN's simplicity. Its processing inefficiency during prediction is one of its main drawbacks. The method can be sluggish and computationally expensive for large datasets since it must determine the distance between each training instance and the test instance in order to identify the closest neighbors. Using compelling data structures like KD-trees or Ball-trees, which can expedite the search for nearest neighbors, can help to some extent ameliorate this problem.

The k-NN's susceptibility to the dimensionality curse is another drawback. It gets harder to discern between the closest and farthest neighbors as the number of dimensions rises because the distance between data points tends to become more consistent. The k-NN algorithm's performance in high-dimensional spaces may be negatively impacted by this issue. Feature selection and dimensionality reduction methods, like t-distributed Stochastic Neighbor Embedding (t-SNE) or Principal

Component Analysis (PCA), are frequently used to solve this problem and enhance k-NN performance.

K-NN is still a valuable and popular method in spite of these drawbacks, especially in situations where simplicity and interpretability are crucial. In domains like image recognition, where it can categorize images according to their pixel intensities or feature vectors obtained from deeper representations, it is frequently used. To provide individualized recommendations, recommendation systems employ k-NN to identify products that bear resemblance to previously appreciated things by the user. Based on sequence similarity or expression levels, genes and proteins are categorized in bioinformatics.

In summary, k-Nearest Neighbors, or k-NN, is a foundational machine learning method that is renowned for its interpretability, adaptability, and simplicity. As a non-parametric approach, it can be used for different data distributions and classifies examples according to the majority vote of their closest neighbors. Even though it has drawbacks such as sensitivity to high-dimensional data and processing inefficiency, these may frequently be minimized with the proper methods. The continued acceptance of k-NN across a range of areas attests to its usefulness and efficiency in resolving real-world issues.

Decision trees and random forests

Two well-known and frequently applied methods in machine learning for classification and regression applications are decision trees and random forests. Due to their interpretability, versatility, and ability to handle big datasets, both approaches have special benefits. Gaining knowledge about the workings and uses of these algorithms can help one appreciate their efficacy and versatility across a range of fields.

A decision tree model represents decisions and their possible outcomes, such as chance event outcomes, resource costs, and utility, using a graph that resembles a tree. A tree structure representing a "test" on an attribute for each internal node, the result of the test for each branch, and the class label (or continuous value in the case of regression) for each leaf node is the result of recursively partitioning the data into subsets based on the value of input features. Partitioning keeps going until the tree gets to a certain depth, or until every data item in a node is in the same class, or until any other conditions are satisfied. The major objective is to create a model that forecasts the target variable using fundamental decision rules inferred from the properties of the data.

The interpretability of decision trees is one of their key benefits. The decision-making process can be simply visualized because to the tree structure, which also makes it simple to comprehend and clarify how predictions are made. This functionality is especially helpful in industries like banking and healthcare where transparency is essential. Furthermore, without requiring a lot of preparation, decision trees are adaptable and can handle both numerical and categorical data.

There are, however, a few noteworthy disadvantages with decision trees. A tree that grows too deeply is more likely to overfit and identify noise in the training set as patterns rather than the underlying ones. To lessen this problem, pruning techniques—which entail cutting off portions of the tree that don't provide more predictive power—are frequently employed. Decision trees can also be unstable since slight alterations in the input might produce noticeably different tree architectures. Another disadvantage is that it is sensitive to changes in the training data.

The random forest algorithm was created in order to overcome these restrictions. During training, a random forest is an ensemble learning strategy that creates many decision trees and calculates the mean prediction (regression) or class mode (classification) for each tree separately. This method makes use of the phenomenon known as ensemble learning, in which the combined judgment of several models frequently outperforms the judgment of a single model. Every tree in a random forest is constructed utilizing a randomly selected portion of the training data that is chosen by replacement (a process called bagging). Random forests also take into account a random subset of features when splitting nodes, which adds further variability and lowers the correlation between individual trees.

Compared to single decision trees, random forests provide a number of advantages. By averaging the predictions across several trees, they first considerably lower the chance of overfitting, producing a more reliable and broadly applicable model. Due to the ensemble approach's ability to mix the advantages of different trees, they also increase accuracy. Third, random forests offer a feature importance metric that may be used to determine which variables in the dataset have the most influence. This feature is beneficial for selecting features and comprehending the underlying data structure.

Random forests have advantages, but they also have certain drawbacks. Because numerous trees must be built and maintained, they need more computing resources than a single decision tree, both in terms of memory and processing power. When dealing with highly massive datasets or when computing resources are few, this could be a disadvantage. Furthermore, random forests provide some insights into the decision-making process of the model through feature importance metrics, albeit being less interpretable than single decision trees.

Random forests and decision trees have a wide range of uses. They are employed in finance for fraud detection, risk assessment, and credit scoring. These algorithms are used in the medical field for disease diagnosis, patient outcome prediction, and probable treatment plan identification. They support churn prediction, tailored recommendations, and consumer segmentation in marketing. Furthermore, random forests are widely employed in bioinformatics for applications like protein function prediction and gene expression analysis.

To sum up, decision trees and random forests are robust machine learning methods with a variety of uses and benefits. Decision trees are prized for being easily understood and explicable due to their simplicity and interpretability. Their sensitivity to fluctuations in the data and tendency to overfit, however, may restrict their usefulness. By averaging the forecasts of several trees, random forests, as an ensemble method, address these problems and produce more reliable and accurate models. Even though random forests are more complicated to understand and need more processing power than single decision trees, their feature importance metrics nevertheless yield insightful information. These algorithms' broad application across numerous domains attests to their adaptability and potency in resolving practical issues.

CHAPTER VIII

Ensemble Methods

Bagging and boosting

Two well-known ensemble learning strategies in machine learning, bagging, and boosting, combine several weak learners to produce a strong learner with the goal of enhancing model performance and robustness. While improving forecast accuracy is the common aim of these techniques, their methodology and approach are very different. They comprehend the subtleties of bagging and boosting and offer a valuable understanding of their efficacy in diverse applications, encompassing tasks such as regression and classification.

Leo Breiman introduced the concept of Bagging, which stands for Bootstrap Aggregating, in 1996. Using diverse subsets of the training data to train several copies of the same algorithm is intended to lower the variance of a prediction model. By using replacement sampling to sample the dataset at random, a technique known as bootstrapping, these subsets are produced. For regression tasks, the final prediction is determined by averaging the predictions, and for classification tasks, it is determined by a majority vote. Each subset is used to train a different model, usually a decision tree. The main idea behind bagging is to produce a variety of models that each capture a distinct feature of the data, therefore avoiding overfitting and lowering the overall variance. All of the models in the ensemble have a somewhat different viewpoint on the data thanks to the randomization that bootstrapping introduces, which results in more consistent and accurate predictions overall.

Boosting, on the other hand, trains models progressively, with each new model aiming to fix the mistakes of the preceding ones, with the goal of minimizing both bias and variance. Boosting doesn't rely on random sampling with replacement like bagging does. Instead, it modifies the training instance weights according to how accurately they are classified. Every instance has the same weight at first, but in every iteration, the cases that were incorrectly classified have heavier weights, which makes them more noticeable when training the subsequent model. This procedure guarantees that the new model concentrates more on the challenging cases that were mislabeled in the past. In boosting, the ultimate forecast is a weighted total of all the models' predictions, with more accurate models producing a larger final output. Two popular boosting techniques are Gradient Boosting and AdaBoost (Adaptive Boosting). AdaBoost modifies the weights of incorrectly categorized cases directly, whereas Gradient Boosting minimizes a loss function using gradient descent, progressively increasing the model's accuracy.

Their benefits are evident in the performance boosts that bagging and boosting yield on a range of machine learning applications. Bagging is especially useful for reducing overfitting and stabilizing high-variance models, such as decision trees, by averaging out the predictions. Because of this, bagging works effectively in scenarios when the model has a tendency to overfit the training set. An extension of bagging, Random Forest is a well-liked ensemble technique that mixes numerous decision trees. Random Forest improves the performance and diversity of the ensemble by training each tree on a distinct collection of attributes. By concentrating on the mistakes made by earlier models, boosting, on the other hand, is excellent at turning weak learners into strong ones. By using a sequential technique, boosting makes it possible to build exact models that can recognize intricate patterns in the data. Strong boosting algorithms like Gradient Boosting Machines (GBM) and eXtreme Gradient Boosting (XGBoost) have proven effective in a number of data science competitions and real-world applications.

Despite their advantages, boosting and bagging have certain drawbacks. Even though it works well to lower variance, bagging ignores the model's bias. Scooping up several instances of a biased base learner won't make a big difference in performance if that's the case. Furthermore, because bagging necessitates the independent training of many models, it demands additional computer power. Despite its strength, boosting is susceptible to noise and anomalies in the training set. Boosting may overemphasize noisy data since it concentrates on difficult-to-classify cases, which can result in overfitting. Furthermore, because boosting techniques necessitate iterative training and meticulous hyperparameter adjustment, they are typically more intricate and computationally demanding.

Boosting and bagging have a wide range of uses. These methods are applied in finance to stock price prediction, fraud detection, and credit scoring. They support disease diagnosis, prognostication of patient outcomes, and individualized treatment strategies in the healthcare industry. Bagging and boosting algorithms are used in marketing for targeted advertising, churn prediction, and customer segmentation. They are employed in sentiment analysis, machine translation, and text classification in natural language processing. These ensemble methods' adaptability enables them to be used in a variety of contexts, frequently resulting in notable increases in model robustness and predictive accuracy.

To sum up, by merging several weak learners, bagging and boosting are two essential ensemble learning strategies that improve the performance of machine learning models. While boosting decreases bias and variation through sequential training and error correction, bagging reduces variance through bootstrapping and parallel training. Every technique has advantages and disadvantages; bagging works better for high-variance models while boosting works best for turning poor learners into strong predictors. These methods' wide range of applications in various domains attests to their significance and potency in handling challenging predicting jobs. Understanding and applying the bagging and boosting ideas can greatly enhance machine learning models, leading to more dependable and accurate predictions.

Random forests

In machine learning, random forests are a flexible and effective ensemble learning technique that is often applied to classification and regression problems. Random forests are an ensemble technique that improves the prediction performance and robustness of decision trees. They were created by Leo Breiman and Adele Cutler in the early 2000s. Due to its capacity to handle big datasets, control high-dimensional spaces, and generate precise predictions while reducing the overfitting issue that decision trees are frequently known for, this approach has seen a considerable increase in popularity.

A collection of decision trees, or "forest," forms the basis of a random forest. Random forests represent the principle of ensemble learning, which is predicated on the notion that a collection of weak learners can be united to generate a powerful learner. Decision trees are weak learners in the context of random forests. Using a technique known as bootstrap sampling, an independent portion of the training data is chosen for each tree before it is built in the forest. This implies that a distinct random sample of the data is taken with replacement for every tree. As a result, specific data points might be included again in the sample while others might not. This method adds variation amongst the individual trees.

Random forests select a random subset of features at each decision tree split, adding another layer of unpredictability on top of bootstrap sampling. The unpredictability of the features guarantees that every tree examines various patterns and interactions in the data, hence augmenting the variety of the trees. Random forests can lower the variance of the model and enhance its capacity for generalization by combining the predictions of several trees. Majority voting is commonly used in classification tasks to determine the final prediction. Each tree casts a vote for a class label, and the label with the most votes is selected. The final result for regression tasks is calculated by averaging the predictions of each individual tree.

When compared to individual decision trees, the random forest method has a number of advantages. The main benefit is in its capacity to reduce overfitting. When decision trees get large and complicated, they often overfit the training set. Random forests smooth down the noise and variability found in individual trees by averaging the outcomes of numerous trees, producing a more reliable and broadly applicable model. The ensemble approach performs particularly well when dealing with datasets that are noisy or contain a large number of extraneous features.

The effectiveness with which random forests can handle high-dimensional data is another critical benefit. Large datasets with plenty of features can be processed by the technique without requiring a lot of feature selection or preparation. By prohibiting any one feature from controlling the decision-making process, the random feature selection at each split lowers the danger of overfitting and guarantees that the model is still computationally feasible. Because of this property, random forests can be used for a variety of tasks, such as financial modeling, genetic data analysis, and the classification of text and images.

In addition, random forests offer an intrinsic feature importance metric that is helpful in deciphering the data's underlying structure and pinpointing the variables that have the most impact. The reduction in the model's performance when a feature's values are permuted can be used to determine how important a feature is. If the values of features that are important to the accuracy of the model are changed, the model's performance will suffer dramatically. This knowledge can influence feature selection, enhance the interpretability of the model, and help with domain-specific decision-making.

Even with their advantages, random forests have drawbacks. Their memory consumption and computational complexity are two significant disadvantages. It might take a lot of resources to train and store numerous decision trees, especially for massive datasets. Although this problem can be lessened by employing effective data structures and parallel processing strategies, random forests should still be used with caution in situations where resources are limited. Furthermore, random forests are typically less transparent than single decision trees despite the fact that they provide some interpretability through feature importance metrics. Individual decisions are less interpretable due to the ensemble aspect of the model, which can be a drawback in situations where model transparency is essential.

Random forests have been widely used in many different fields. They are employed in finance for automated trading, fraud detection, and credit scoring. Random forests are used in healthcare to help with medical picture processing, patient outcome prediction, and illness identification. They support recommendation engines, churn prediction, and consumer segmentation in marketing. For many machine learning practitioners and researchers, the method is the first choice because of its robustness and capacity to handle complicated datasets.

To sum up, random forests are a potent and adaptable machine learning method that makes use of ensemble learning's advantages to generate reliable and accurate models. Random forests work by mixing numerous decision trees that were trained on random subsets of the data and features. This helps to manage high-dimensional data, reduce overfitting, and offer insightful information about the significance of individual features. Their importance in the machine learning landscape is underscored by their ubiquitous applicability and effectiveness in many disciplines despite certain computational constraints and interpretability issues. Predictive modeling and data analysis can significantly advance an understanding of and application for random forests.

CONCLUSION

Is a thorough and insightful examination of the rapidly evolving domains of artificial intelligence, data science, and machine learning. This book explores in great detail the fundamental ideas, real-world uses, and potential long-term effects of this quickly developing technology. The book effectively demystifies complex subjects and makes them understandable for both inexperienced readers and seasoned professionals through its comprehensive and readable narrative.

The first step in the trip is a thorough analysis of the basic ideas that machine learning is built upon. With great care, the writers dissect the subtleties of algorithms, data preprocessing, and model validation, giving readers a firm foundation in the fundamentals of machine learning. This background information is essential because it gives readers the skills necessary to comprehend more complex subjects and interact critically with the text.

The book's practical focus is one of its most vital points. The writers stress the practical uses of data science and machine learning, using examples and case studies from a range of businesses to highlight key ideas. This sensible approach not only improves understanding but also shows how these technologies affect daily living. The book regularly links theoretical principles to practical outcomes, highlighting the relevance and value of machine learning and artificial intelligence. Examples of these applications include recommendation systems in e-commerce, autonomous systems in transportation, and predictive analytics in healthcare.

The book also is open when discussing the moral and societal ramifications of these technologies. The writers offer a fair viewpoint in an environment where concerns about algorithmic unfairness, data privacy, and the possibility of job displacement are urgent. They discuss the moral issues that come with technology development and promote the ethical and just application of data science and artificial intelligence. The writers' awareness of the larger environment in which these technologies function is demonstrated by this thoughtful discussion.

The book's futuristic portions, which forecast machine learning and artificial intelligence's future paths, are exciting. The writers discuss new developments that could influence the future, highlighting topics including sophisticated neural networks, quantum computing, and reinforcement learning. They also talk about how AI could transform a number of industries, like climate modeling and personalized medicine, giving us a hopeful but grounded outlook for the future.

It's important to note that "Machine Learning Unraveled" is distinguished by its clarity and accessibility. The authors make sure that complicated ideas are presented in an exciting and approachable way by carefully balancing technical complexity with readability. For this reason, the book is an invaluable resource for a broad readership that includes academics, instructors, professionals in business, and inquisitive laypeople.

To sum up, "Machine Learning Unraveled: Exploring the World of Data Science and AI" is a superb synthesis of the theoretical underpinnings, real-world uses, and potential future paths of AI and machine learning. Anyone interested in these revolutionary technologies should read it because of its thorough coverage, useful insights, ethical issues, and forward-thinking viewpoints. By bridging the gap between complexity and accessibility, the book not only teaches readers but also inspires them to explore and contribute to the rapidly evolving fields of data science and artificial intelligence. As we approach unparalleled technological breakthroughs, this book urges readers to navigate and shape the future with knowledge, accountability, and curiosity. It also acts as a spark for invention.

Thank you for buying and reading/ listening to our book. If you found this book useful/ helpful please take a few minutes and leave a review on the platform where you purchased our book. Your feedback matters greatly to us.

www.ingramcontent.com/pod-product-compliance
Lightning Source LLC
Chambersburg PA
CBHW071527150726
48000CB00002B/716